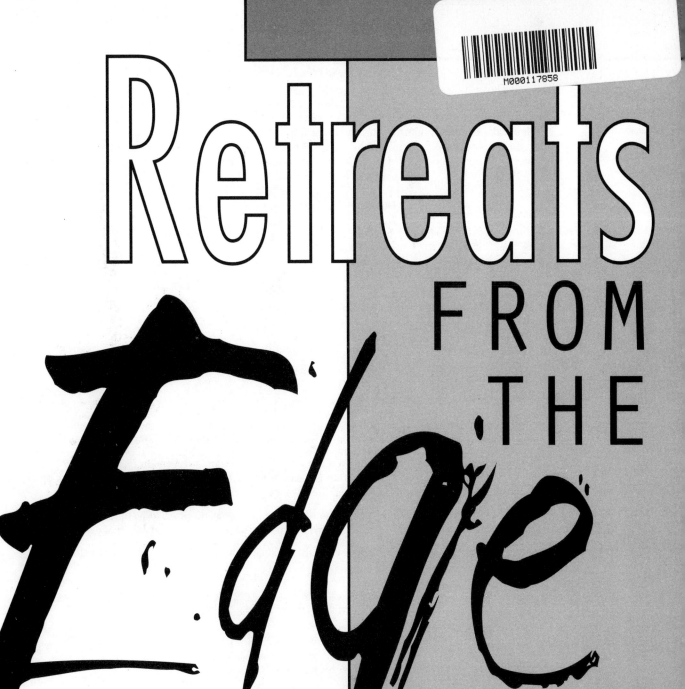

Retreats FROM THE Edge

Youth Events to Build A Christian Community

by Paul Harcey and The Edge Ministries

ABINGDON PRESS
Nashville

RETREATS FROM THE EDGE
Youth Events to Build a Christian Community

Copyright © 1998 by Abingdon Press

This book is printed on recycled paper.

Library of Congress Cataloging-in-Publication Data

Harcey, Paul, 1968-
   Retreats from the Edge: youth events to build a Christian community /
Paul Harcey and the Edge Ministries.
       80p.   cm.—(Essentials for Christian youth)
    ISBN 0-687-07581-5 (pbk.: alk. paper)
    1. Retreats for youth. I. Edge Ministries. II. Title.
III. Series.
BV4447.H2948 1998
269′.63—dc21   97-40914
                                                                                    CIP

Scripture quotations in this publication, unless otherwise indicated, are from the *Contemporary English Version,* Copyright © 1991, 1992, 1995 by American Bible Society. Used by permission.

Scripture quotations noted NRSV are from the New Revised Standard Version of the Bible copyrighted © 1989 by the Division of Christian Education of the National Council of the Churches of Christ in the United States of America, and are used by permission. All rights reserved.

The purpose of RETREATS FROM THE EDGE is to help youth thrive as disciples of Jesus Christ by providing extended programs that encourage physical, relational, emotional, and spiritual growth.

Purchase of one copy of this book conveys to the local church the right to reproduce handouts as herein indicated.

98 99 00 01 02 03 04 05 06 07—10 9 8 7 6 5 4 3 2 1

Designers: Diana Maio and Phillip D. Francis
Cover design by Diana Maio
Cover art by Dennas Davis
Back cover photo courtesy of The Edge Ministries

MANUFACTURED IN THE UNITED STATES OF AMERICA

ACKNOWLEDGEMENTS

RETREATS FROM THE EDGE was a team effort; many different authors put these retreats together. I would like to acknowledge everyone who had a part in developing and producing this resource. My thanks go to
   • God for bringing together the people who started The Edge Ministries and the many others who have joined us throughout our ministry life;
   • Tony Peterson and Abingdon Press for editing and publishing this resource;
   • the many groups who have put their faith on the Edge and have given me a place to minister;
   • the writers of and contributors to this book: Matt Charlton, Brandon Dirks, Leif Dove, Ashley Dusenbery, Duke Gatsos, Jon Joy, Rick McNeeley, and Mary Schulze.

—**Paul Harcey**
Staff Executive of The Edge Ministries

Table of Contents

INTRODUCTION

ABOUT THE EDGE

All the ideas in this book have been road-tested across the country with The Edge Ministries. The Edge is a flexible ministry organization that trys to respond to the needs of each group we work with. Through adventure activities such as rappelling, climbing, camping, and rope courses, we push students physically, mentally, and emotionally. Then we lead worship and study sessions to help youth look at the Bible in new ways that will push them spiritually. The Edge tries to create a safe environment for growth. For more information or to use our services, contact us at

The Edge Ministries
P.O. Box 850
Antioch, TN 37013

Voice mail: 615-731-EDGE (3343)
e-mail: edge3343@aol.com

ABOUT RETREATS FROM THE EDGE

Inside you will find retreats full of ideas that you can use with your youth group. This resource features the same flexibility that characterizes The Edge Ministries. In each retreat you will find study sessions, worship services or devotions, ideas for games, and a suggested schedule. Use the ideas in any way that will work for your group.

ABOUT THE ADVENTURE

☛ We encourage your group to go to an adventure camp or other outdoor location for these retreats. Although most of the activities are transferable to various settings, the best results will come from outdoor surroundings. Where the afternoon schedule calls for free time, you might opt to insert climbing or hiking opportunities.

☛ You may not have access to a location that would allow climbing on a rockface. A suggested alternative to the day of outdoor climbing (see "Hitting Solid Rock: Jesus Christ," page 19) would be a day of indoor climbing. Due to the increasing popularity of rock climbing, many cities now have indoor climbing gyms. The challenging routes and helpful instructors offered by these gyms ensure the interest and safety of all participants. Group rates are available at most climbing gyms.

☛ If you are not able to get "on rope," you can still experience the challenge of rock climbing through the climbing style known as "bouldering." Traditional rock climbing is a horizontal ascent of a rockface. Bouldering is a vertical traverse never reaching more than a few feet from the ground. Spotters are used to make sure participants do not get hurt if they fall.

Warning: Rock climbing is inherently dangerous and should not be attempted without the assistance and guidance of climbers who have been trained to lead others in climbing. If you do not know what you are doing, or if you do not have access to persons who know what they are doing, DON'T CLIMB. But *do* hire experienced instructors. It just so happens that the authors of this book know what they are doing. To hire us, see our contact information on page 4.

ABOUT LEADING RETREATS

☛ Planning is the key.

☛ All retreats require preparation. We want to make that preparation easy for you. First, think about your group:

- Describe the group as it currently exists.
- In what areas would you like to see your group grow?
- How would you like the group to "look" after the retreat?
- What steps will you take to accomplish this goal?

☛ Choose a particular retreat and read through the program description. Make notes about these items:

- materials needed
- ways to prepare
- concerns for your group

ABOUT MUSIC

In RETREATS FROM THE EDGE, we suggest music primarily as a part of worship. In most cases we recommend specific songs. Feel free to use our recommendations or to use songs that you know will work with your group. Our suggestions come primarily from two albums that are available on both cassette and CD: *Youth! Praise 3: Jesus Is the Rock* and *Songs,* by Rich Mullins.

Those titles designated with a plus sign (+) are from *Youth! Praise 3: Jesus Is the Rock* (Abingdon Press, 1995). The cassette and CD include tracks with and without vocals, so that your group can sing along. The CD comes complete with CD Graphics so that words can be displayed for group singing. Available from your local Cokesbury bookstore or other Christian bookstore. Cassette: $9.95, 0-687-01758-0; CD: $13.95, 0-687-01759-9.

Those titles designated with an equal sign (=) are from *Songs,* by Rich Mullins (Reunion Records, 1996). Available through your local Cokesbury bookstore or a record store. Cassette: $10.98; CD: $16.98.

ABOUT GAMES

We suggest various games in these outlines. This resource lists and describes all the games, starting with page 76. Expect some games to flop; they are not all winners with every group. Be flexible in your planning. Prepare for more activities than you think you will need. Have all your supplies ready to go.

A FEW DEFINITIONS

One-on-One Time
One-on-one time is designed for personal morning devotions. We have included time for devotions in each retreat outline. In a few cases we include our original devotions; but mostly we have allowed you the option of creating your own to fit your group. We use one-on-one time in each retreat we conduct; we recommend that you do the same.

Loopy Time
Loopy time is...time to get loopy! The Edge created a caricature called Mr. Loopy, who gets to lead all the games and crazy songs on a retreat. If you do not wish to bring Mr. Loopy to life, then just lead games in your own fun and crazy way. Fun is a valid part of any retreat (it may even be the main reason some participants are attending the event).

Laying the Foundation

WHAT'S THE POINT?

This retreat is an opportunity for the participants to make future plans for the group. All members should be as involved as possible in the day-to-day and long-range planning of the group. The ownership they gain from preparing for their year together is invaluable. We recommend that you plan for at least six months ahead (a year ahead is even better).

WHY IT MATTERS

"For I know the plans I have for you," declares the LORD, "plans to prosper you and not to harm you, plans to give you hope and a future. Then you will call upon me and come and pray to me, and I will listen to you. You will seek me and find me when you seek me with all your heart" (Jeremiah 29:11-13, New International Version).

OTHER SCRIPTURE REFERENCES IN THIS RETREAT

Genesis 6:8-22
Romans 12:1-2

Retreat Schedule

Friday Night

7:00	Arrive and unpack
7:30	Loopy time
8:15	Review expectations for the weekend
8:30	Break
8:45	Brainwarmer games
9:15	Session 1
10:30	Worship
11:00	Lights out

Saturday

8:00	Breakfast
8:30	One-on-one time
9:00	Session 2
10:00	Break
10:30	More priorities
12:00	Lunch
12:30	Session 3
1:15	Break
2:30	Free time
6:00	Dinner
7:00	Session 4
9:00	Free time
11:00	Lights out

Sunday

8:00	Breakfast
8:30	One-on-one time
9:00	Finalize calendars
9:45	Break and pack-up
10:30	Dedication Service
11:30	Depart

FRIDAY NIGHT

Before the first session, try some brain warm-ups. We suggest "Jump the Peg," to start. That game and some other options appear on pages 76 and 77.

SESSION 1: EVALUATION

Start with prayer, asking God to be present and to guide the evaluation process.

☛ Lead a short Bible study on Genesis 6. Hand out copies of the "Ark of the Future" worksheet (page 10). Work through the questions.

☛ Briefly outline the process of the retreat. Introduce the four areas of concentration—evaluation, setting priorities, brainstorming, and calendaring— so that the youth get a sense of how everything ties together. Encourage a spirit of good intentions for this retreat. The goal is to help the group move forward by reviewing the past.

☛ Begin a discussion of the importance of evaluation. Ask these questions:

  • Why is it important to look back on the past year?
  • How do we make sure we don't repeat the same mistakes?
  • Have you ever made similar mistakes over and over?

☛ Remember and evaluate past activities. Distribute copies of the "Memories" and "Activities" evaluation page. Have everyone fill out each portion.

☛ Collect the evaluation forms to use as a starting point for the "Setting Priorities" session on Saturday.

FRIDAY NIGHT WORSHIP

☛ *Opening Prayer*: Invite God to be present, and ask that the participants be open to hearing something new about God.

☛ *Song*: Choose a song that invites the coming of the Holy Spirit (for example, +"You Make Your Home in Me").

☛ *Scripture*: Have someone read aloud Jeremiah 29:11-13.

☛ *Message*: Take about five minutes to encourage receptivity to a new way of doing things. Also invite creativity. Remind the group members that they are here to dream of what could be.

☛ *Offering*: Have each person write down one change he or she thinks the group needs to make. The youth are also to write down one thing they appreciate most about the group. Have them bring these items to the altar as a symbol that they are offering their ideas to God. As the youth are writing, you may want to play some upbeat worship music in the background (for example, a selection from *Songs,* by Rich Mullins).

☛ *Closing Prayer*: Pray that God will help make the group's ideas and plans a reality. Give thanks for the ability to explore new possibilities and dream dreams.

SATURDAY

SESSION 2: SETTING PRIORITIES

☛ Before this session, review the evaluations and note any trends.

☛ Begin the session with prayer. If you wish, have someone lead a short devotion, linking the one-on-one times with setting priorities.

☛ Introduce the session. Inform the participants that during the next session they will help decide the direction the group is going to take. Issues to consider will include the needs of the group, the wants of the group, and the mission of the group. (For the format of this session, we are indebted to Ron Loewen.)

☛ Ask this question:

  • What are the current needs of our group, community, and church that are not being met?

☛ Write down some of the answers to this question on a large sheet of paper. (Possible responses: Some members of the group are being excluded, we don't worship often enough, our plans always fall through.)

☞ Add any trends the evaluation process provided.

☞ Arrange the responses in order of priority. Give each person three red adhesive dots and ten blue dots. Say something like: "Place red dots beside the items that you feel are most important. Use the blue dots to indicate items you agree with, but don't necessarily feel passionate about. You may put as many or as few dots by each answer as you wish."

☞ After all the dots have been affixed, count them and display the totals.

☞ Come to a consensus. Establish several priorities (two to five) for the six-month (or longer) period for which you are planning. While the response with the most dots is probably the most important, discuss each item to make sure that the whole group can accept the total list. Record on a large sheet of paper the priorities the group agrees to observe for the next six months.

☞ End with a prayer.

SESSION 3: BRAINSTORMING

During this session, the group will identify actions and activities that are crucial to accomplishing their priorities. The central question for the process is, How are we going to accomplish our priorities for the year?

☞ Start with a prayer.

☞ To ensure balanced programming, break down the brainstorming activity into the ministry areas listed below. Have the group work in teams of up to six persons. Give each team a sheet of paper with one of the five areas listed at the top. Allow about five minutes for the teams to come up with as many ideas as they can for each area. At the end of the time, have the teams exchange sheets and add any suggestions they may have that relate to the new priority they are considering. Continue until each group has had a chance to talk about each priority.

> *Worship*
> *Service*
> *Study*
> *Fellowship*
> *Outreach*

☞ During a short break before this next segment, take time to transfer the information on all the smaller sheets of paper to a large sheet of paper. If you have a large group, consider doing some preliminary setting of priorities before involving the whole group.

☞ Once again establish priorities. Use the dot method of prioritizing if you like, or just try to reach a consensus with the group. The goal is to leave the session with a list of activities that can be recorded on a calendar during the next session. The number of activities the group can do will be limited by such factors as time, resources, and energy. Set a number beforehand—something like two a month for each priority, or one activity in each ministry area a month (making sure that you hit each priority).

☞ End the session with a prayer.

SESSION 4: SETTING THE CALENDAR

During this session, you will record the suggested activities on a calendar. Also note significant dates that appear on the church calendar as well as dates for important school activities. If the group is large, you may choose to complete the calendar part with a smaller group, something like a youth council.

☞ Begin the session with a prayer.

☞ Talk to the group about flexibility. Emphasize that while it is good to remain flexible, the work done during this retreat will be a waste of time if everything ends up being changed later.

☞ Use these tips for the calendar session:

• Start by recording the big events and trips first.
• Don't fill in only one type of activity at a time. If you record all the fellowship activities first, you eventually may run out of dates for the service projects.
• If necessary, take a few breaks. Matching dates with projects can be a tedious process. Consider leaving some of the work for Sunday. Or you may want to revisit the process on another day.

SUNDAY

DEDICATION SERVICE

Use this worship segment to dedicate the group's plans to God.

☛ *Opening Song*: Set a worshipful mood with music.

☛ *Opening Prayer*: Invite the Holy Spirit's presence.

☛ *Offerings*: Have several different youth bring the group's priorities, activities, and calendar to the altar. Invite each person to say a few words of dedication to God, such as: "God, we bring you our priorities; may they reflect your will for our group. Help us translate them into reality."

☛ **Sing or play a song** that will help people think about their commitment to Jesus Christ and to the group, such as + "John 12:26: Follow Me."

☛ *Scripture*: Have someone read aloud Romans 12:1 and 2.

☛ *Message*: Issue a challenge to the group to live out what God has called them to be. Urge the youth to begin a closer walk with Jesus Christ. Challenge each person to embrace the plans of the group and to be personally involved in bringing about the kingdom of God.

☛ *Prayer*: Ask God to go with the group and to help bring about what may sometimes seem humanly impossible.

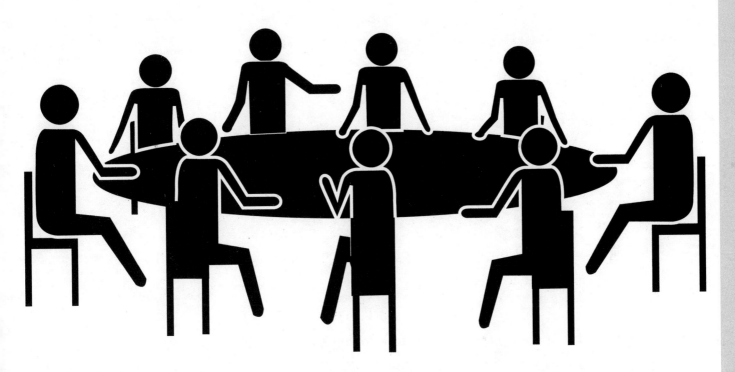

Ark of the Future

Read aloud Genesis 6:8-22, then discuss these questions:

1. Why, do you think, did God choose Noah?

2. Why, do you think, did God give Noah such specific instructions?

3. What did God promise to Noah?

4. What did Noah have to do, if anything, to receive God's reward?

5. Do you feel chosen by God? Do you know if you are chosen? Explain.

6. Do you think God has specific plans for you? How do you know?

7. What might you have to do to follow God's plans?

8. What might your reward be?

Worksheets

Memories

Write down your best memories of time spent with the youth group during the past year. Try to be as specific as possible (where you were, what was going on, and so forth).

What, do you think, made the good experiences so memorable? Try to list a number of factors. Think about all the possible elements that helped create a special atmosphere or mood.

Activities

1. What was your favorite youth activity over the past year? Why?

2. What was your least favorite? Why?

3. Write down the four most meaningful youth events or activities of the year.

4. Write down the four least meaningful youth events or activities of the year.

5. What do you think needs to change about the group?

6. What is your favorite characteristic of the group?

7. Of these five areas—fellowship, service, worship, outreach, study—which do you think we need to concentrate on more? Why?

Living on the Edge: Trust

WHAT'S THE POINT?

Trust is at the core of all relationships, including our relationship with God. This essential foundation of any group is hard to build and easy to destroy. Still, we need to trust one another with our ideas, thoughts, dreams, and problems. More important, we need to trust that God will lead us, help us, and love us no matter what. This retreat offers hands-on activities and discussion outlines to lay the foundation of trust within your group.

WHY IT MATTERS

"I depend on you, / and I have trusted you since I was young. / I have relied on you from the day I was born. / You brought me safely through birth, / and I always praise you" (Psalm 71:5-6).

OTHER SCRIPTURE REFERENCES IN THIS RETREAT

Psalm 25:1-7
Psalm 40
Micah 5:2b-5
Matthew 1:22-25
Matthew 6:19-21, 25-34
John 15:1-9

Retreat Schedule

Friday Night

7:00	Arrive and settle in
7:30	Expectations for the weekend
8:15	Loopy time
8:30	Break
9:00	Session 1
10:00	Break
10:30	Worship
11:00	Bed prep time

Saturday

7:00	Wake up
7:30	Breakfast
9:00	Loopy time
9:30	Session 2
11:00	Free time
12:00	Lunch
1:30	Session 3
4:00	Free time
6:00	Supper
7:30	Worship
9:00	Break
9:30	Campfire
11:30	Bed prep time
12:00	Lights out

Sunday

7:00	Wake up
7:30	Breakfast
9:00	Loopy time
9:30	Clean and pack up
11:00	Worship

FRIDAY NIGHT

SESSION 1: WHAT IS TRUST?

Preparation: Make copies of the "Trust Questions" worksheet. On a large sheet of paper, write several dictionary definitions of the word *trust* (include at least the first three definitions that you find listed). Post several blank large sheets of paper (*do not post the definitions yet*).

☛ Prayer: Ask God to be a part of the group's experience together.

☛ Ask: What is trust? Write the responses on a blank sheet of paper.

☛ Say: "Let's think about what the dictionary says about trust." Post the dictionary definitions. Compare the definitions with some of the words and concepts suggested by the group.

☛ Hand out the "Trust Questions" worksheets and give the youth a few minutes to fill them out.

☛ Invite volunteers to tell what they wrote. Write some of the responses on a posted sheet of paper.

☛ Record on a large sheet of paper under the heading "Qualities," the responses to why certain people are trusted.

☛ Say something like: "When we want to experience trust, we should show ourselves to be trustworthy." Then ask:

• What does it mean to be trustworthy?
• How do we build trust?
• What do you want our group to get out of this session as we think about trust?

FRIDAY NIGHT WORSHIP

The focus of this service is the worship of the God who is worthy of our trust.

Preparation: Gather eight index cards. Write "Promise Made" at the top of four cards; on each of these four, write one of the Bible verses in that category. Write "Promise Kept" at the top of four other cards and add the corresponding verses, one to a card. Choose up to eight readers ahead of time.

Promises Made	Promises Kept
1. Genesis 2:18	1. Genesis 2:21-24
2. Genesis 6:13	2. Genesis 7:17-24
3. Exodus 3:7-10	3. Exodus 12:31-32
4. Micah 5:2-5	4. Matthew 1:22-25

☛ *Prayer:* "Dear God, the Bible tells us that you have a perfect track record with us humans. You always come through on everything that you promise. Enable us to trust you in our daily life. Help us build our trust into a strong faith in you and what you can do in our life."

☛ *Songs:* Use these or other songs that deal with following or trusting God: +"Lean On," "Take My Hand," "Psalm 71."

☛ *Scripture:* Invite the readers to read aloud their Bible passages. (Have the first reader say "promise made," and read aloud Genesis 2:18; then have the second reader say "promise kept," and read aloud the Genesis 2:21-24 passage. Continue with this pattern.)

☛ *Closing:* Say something like: "All through the Bible, God is revealed as the Creator who keeps promises. God makes promises to all people, especially to followers of Jesus Christ. God promises us strength to live our life. We trust God to supply what we need each day. As in all relationships, trust is the most important ingredient between us and God."

SESSION 2: TRUST VERSUS FAITH

The purpose of this session is to discover both the similarities and the differences between faith and trust.

☛ Start with a couple games, such as "Back-to-Back Partner Stand" or "Everybody Up" (see page 76).

☛ Then say something like: "Today we will look at how trust and faith are alike and yet different."

☛ Review the definitions of trust from Session 1.

☛ Then ask:

- How would you define faith?
- How are faith and trust similar?
- How are faith and trust different?

☛ Then say: "One definition of trust is giving up control and power to someone or something. While you may have faith that a car will run, trust is not evident until you get in and push the gas pedal. You may have faith that God will satisfy your needs; trust is evident when you give God your life."

☛ Have the youth gather in two teams (or teams in multiples of two). Give each team a copy of the "Trust Scenarios" worksheet (page 18). Have the teams read the scenarios; then have one group answer the "Trust" questions and another one answer the "Faith" questions.

☛ Post two large sheets of paper, with the word *faith* written on one and the word *trust* on the other. Invite the participants to give definitions for each word (indicate differences between the two terms). Post a third sheet of paper with the word *similarities* on it. Invite the participants to define this word as well. When you have enough responses on each sheet, close the discussion by summing up the definitions of the three terms.

SESSION 3: TRUST-BUILDING GAMES

The games listed below will give the participants hands-on experience in building trust (see "Games From the Edge," beginning on page 76). Have fun, but maintain safety during these activities. Start with games that require lower levels of trust and move toward higher levels. Most of these activities and games are best done with groups of eight to twelve. Some can be adapted to larger groups if necessary.

Debrief these activities to discover their meaning. Take time after each activity or two to find out what the group is doing well and what can be done better. Find out how the group members are feeling about themselves and the group. At the end of the day, talk with the youth about what they have learned and how it applies to their spiritual and daily life.

WARM-UPS
Everybody Up
Touch This Can
All Aboard
Up Chuck
Under the Fence

MEDIUM TRUST LEVEL
Electric Fence
Minefield
Trust Walk

HIGH TRUST LEVEL
Trust Fall
Willow in the Wind

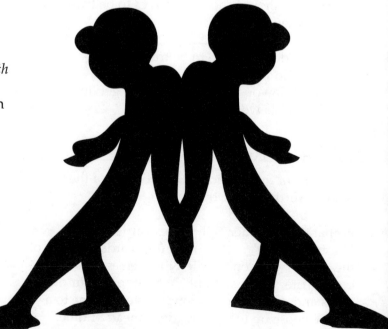

SATURDAY NIGHT WORSHIP

Preparation: Select the cast for a skit based on the story below. You will need a Narrator, a Tightrope Walker, and various crowd members.

☛ *Opening Prayer*

☛ *Call to Worship*: Use any song or liturgy to invite the Spirit.

☛ *Scripture:* Have someone read aloud John 15:1-9.

☛ *Message:* Invite the players to enact the "Faith Skit."

☛ *Explanation*: "Christian faith is actually a matter of trust. This kind of faith means giving your whole life to what you believe. It means 'getting in the basket.' Jesus told the disciples the same thing when he said, 'Abide in me,' or 'Live in me.' Jesus also promises that by living in Christ we will find true life."

☛ Invite the participants to write down on a small piece of paper the part of their life they want to trust God with. Ask them to bring their notes to the altar and to pray that God will receive their gift.

☛ *Song:* Use one having to do with trust, such as + "Psalm 71" or "Take My Life" by Third Day on *Third Day* (Reunion Records).

☛ *Closing Scripture*: Psalm 40

☛ *Closing Prayer*

FAITH SKIT: A man walked a tightrope one hundred feet above Niagara Falls. He started early in the day and walked back and forth many times. As the day wore on, a crowd started to gather. The onlookers were in awe, knowing that if the man slipped even once, he would plunge to his death on the rocks below.

As the crowd grew larger, the man set a bicycle on the wire. He called out to the crowd, "How many of you think I can pedal across the wire on this bike?" The crowd murmured among themselves and finally shouted out, "We have faith that you can do it!" So the man pedaled across and back on the wire twice to prove that he could do it.

Next, he set a basket on the front of the bike and asked again, "How many think I can get across the wire now?" The crowd yelled back, "You can do that easily!" So the man pedaled back and forth on the wire. He then placed a 150-pound rock in the basket and asked, "How many think I can do it now?" The crowd hollered back, "We have faith that you can!" So the man pedaled across and back with the rock in the basket. The man then yelled to the crowd, "I have shown you what I can do. I know that you believe that I can cross this wire with the bike, the basket, and the rock. Who among you trust me enough to ride in the basket yourselves?"

SUNDAY

SUNDAY WORSHIP

Preparation: Invite several youth to create a litany that deals with trusting one another and with having faith in God.

Have some of the group members plan a roleplay using Matthew 6:25-34 as a basis. One person is to play the role of a family member in a modern situation who is consumed with worry and doubt. Have another person talk to the worrier about faith and looking to God for comfort. End the roleplay with someone reading aloud Matthew 6:25-34.

☛ *Litany:* Open worship with the litany created by the youth.

☛ *Scripture:* Have someone read aloud Psalm 25:1-7.

☛ **Prayer:** Ask God to come and be a part of your worship. Thank God for the opportunity to worship the Lord.

☛ *Scripture:* Read aloud Matthew 6:19-21.

☛ *Roleplay:* Have the roleplayers make their presentation based on Matthew 6:25-34.

☛ *Message:* Say something like: "Where we put our energy reflects where our heart is. If we are busy building wealth and storing up possessions, while ignoring God and other people, what good is it? If we do not give of ourselves and do not follow what God has planned, what do we have? When we trust in the Lord and have the faith to follow Jesus Christ, we build up treasures in heaven.

"This weekend we have worked on trusting one another. We have seen how physical trust and spiritual and emotional trust are the same and yet different. Now is the time to go forward to open ourselves to God and others. Although there is a chance we may experience pain, when everything is right, there is growth and healing too."

☛ *Closing Prayer*

Trust Questions

Spend a few minutes answering the following questions about trust.

What is trust?

Is it easy for you to trust others? Why or why not?

Is it easy for others to trust you? Why or why not?

List three people you trust, and why:

Do you trust your teachers?

Do you trust the government?

Do you trust yourself?

Trust Scenarios

❶ Billy's parent is going away for the weekend. He will have the house all to himself while he or she is gone.

❷ Sheila is going away to the beach for her high school senior trip. Roger, her underclassman boyfriend of one year, is not going with her so that she can have fun with her classmates.

❸ Though Martha has some qualms about going to a dance club, she and Beth want to see what it's like and perhaps have a chance to demonstrate their Christian witness. Neither one of them would go to the club without the other one.

❹ God and you begin a relationship of love and friendship.

Questions for each scenario:
GROUP 1—TRUST

1. What might each person expect from the other?

2. How does either person show trust in the other?

3. What things does the person trust the other with?

4. What feelings does the person trust the other with?

5. What might happen if the trust is broken?

6. What could happen if the trust was kept?

GROUP 2—FAITH

1. What might each person expect from the other?

2. What might the persons have faith will happen in their situation?

3. How is either person showing he or she has faith in the other?

4. What qualities may have been displayed by each person that inspired faith on the part of the other?

5. What doubts might either person have to overcome to have faith in the other?

6. What could happen if their faith was misplaced?

7. What could happen if their faith was correct?

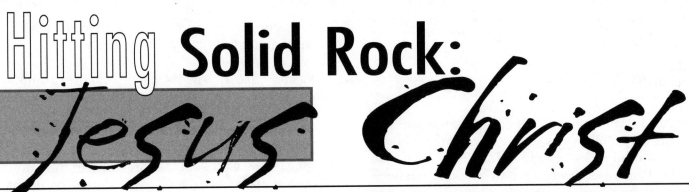

Hitting Solid Rock: Jesus Christ

WHAT'S THE POINT?

This retreat uses the adventure of rock climbing (or other adventure activities) to explore the solid foundation that God lays down for us. The Bible studies revolve around the significance of rocks. Jesus Christ is *the* Rock, the cornerstone of a Christian lifestyle. This dual approach can be a fun, challenging, and meaningful way to experience the Bible as the Word of God.

WHY IT MATTERS

"I patiently waited, LORD, for you to hear my prayer. / You listened and pulled me from a lonely pit full of mud and mire. / You let me stand on a rock with my feet firm"

(Psalm 40:1-2).

OTHER SCRIPTURE REFERENCES IN THIS RETREAT

Genesis 28:10-22
Numbers 20:6-11
Joshua 4:1-8
Psalm 18:1-3
Matthew 16:17-18

Retreat Schedule

Friday Night

7:00	Arrive and unpack
7:30	Loopy time
8:00	Retreat outline and expectations
8:30	Break
9:00	Session 1
10:00	Break
10:30	Worship
11:00	Bed prep
11:30	Lights out

Saturday

7:00	Wake up
8:00	Breakfast/One-on-one time
9:00	Loopy time
10:00	Climbing time
4:00	Back to camp
	—Break
	—Free time
	—Shower
6:00	Dinner
7:30	Loopy time
8:00	Session 2
10:00	Break
10:30	Worship
11:00	Bed prep
11:30	Lights out

Sunday

7:00	Wake up
8:00	Breakfast/One-on-one time
9:00	Loopy time
9:30	Session 3
10:30	Clean up and pack
11:30	Worship

SESSION 1

☛ As everyone gathers, tell the group members that during worship you will be talking about how God used rocks to build a Holy Place. Invite the participants to bring a rock to worship (no mammoth boulders, please!). If you are at a campsite, instruct the participants to remember where they got their rocks. In accordance with the "leave no trace" idea, have them return their rocks to their original resting places when the weekend is over.

☛ Suggested ways to spend this time:

- If someone will later be teaching rock climbing, use this time to start building trust with games (see the "Trust Games" on pages 77 and 78).
- Or use this session for a lesson about rope climbing or knot tying.

☛ At the start of the session or at the end, have one or more persons read aloud the following Scriptures to the group:

> Genesis 28:10-22
> Psalm 40:1-2
> Matthew 16:17-18

Optional Opening
☛ Say: "The Bible uses the words *rock* or *stone* 260 times. Not all references are what one might expect—some are positive, others are negative."

☛ Ask the youth to recall biblical references to a rock or to rocks. Possible anwers:

- stonings
- miracles (David and Goliath, Moses striking the rock)
- sacred places (building altars)
- building walls to keep out enemies
- God or Jesus as the Rock
- protection

☛ Then have the youth form teams of four. Have each team look in the Old Testament for references to rocks or stones. Allow about fifteen minutes. When the participants come back together, have each group give one or two examples. If the following references are not mentioned, offer them and talk about their significance:

Numbers 20:6-11. The people of Israel are grumbling in the desert. God uses a rock to let the people know who is still in control. God tells Moses to strike the rock; when he does, water pours out.

Joshua 4:1-8. God kept the Jordan River from flowing when the Israelites took the ark of the covenant across it. Joshua was instructed to take rocks from the river and build a memorial to the events that happened there.

☛ Close with a reminder to bring a rock to worship.

FRIDAY NIGHT WORSHIP

Preparation: Invite each participant to select a stone and bring it to worship. As the leader, you will need to find a rock that is fairly big. Bring it from home to guarantee having an appropriate one (after the retreat you may leave your rock in your group's meeting room as a reminder of this trip).

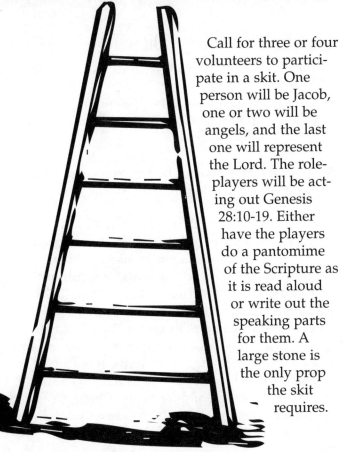

Call for three or four volunteers to participate in a skit. One person will be Jacob, one or two will be angels, and the last one will represent the Lord. The role-players will be acting out Genesis 28:10-19. Either have the players do a pantomime of the Scripture as it is read aloud or write out the speaking parts for them. A large stone is the only prop the skit requires.

☛ *Songs:* Begin worship by singing a few songs that your group likes, such as these selections:

   + "Jesus Is the Rock"
   + "Take My Hand"
   + "Lean On"
   + "As Long As You Are Here With Me"

☛ *Prayer:* Ask God to bless your time of worship; praise God for creation.

☛ *Scripture:* Read aloud Psalm 18:1-3 as a part of your prayer.

☛ *Message:* Introduce the skit by saying something like: "The Bible shows that one of the ways God uses rocks is to mark a place as holy. Piles of rocks were used as altars and monuments." Then invite the actors to present the skit (if they are pantomiming, have someone read aloud Genesis 28:10-19). After the skit invite each person to come forward and place her or his stone in a pile on and around "Jacob's stone." Tell the youth that this pile of stones will mark their place of worship for the rest of the weekend. You will use these rocks again at the end of the weekend.

☛ *Song:* + "As Long As You Are Here With Me"

☛ *Closing Prayer*

SATURDAY

Set this day aside for rock climbing or other adventure activities. For some ideas for other options, call The Edge Ministries at 615-731-EDGE (3343) or e-mail them at edge3343@aol.com.

☛ Start the day with some active warm-up games. "Dragon's Tail" is a good opener (page 79). This activity will help the group members wake up, get their blood moving, and build anticipation.

☛ Trust activities: If you feel that the group is ready for it, do a "Trust Fall" or "Trust Walk" (page 78). The point is that it is necessary to trust one another while climbing.

☛ Once everyone gets to the rocks, lead a devotion with the youth while other leaders set up the site.

☛ Devotion: Have someone read aloud Genesis 1:27-28. Say something like: "God has given us this land and calls us to be the caretakers. Many cultures even consider the land sacred. The land is to be used, managed, and preserved for the benefit of others. Just as you would take care with something you borrowed from a friend, we need to take care of the land that we are borrowing for the time being. We are to be stewards of the land, in these specific ways today:

   • Leave no trace, take only pictures, leave only footprints.
   • Beware of building fires.
   • Do not remove or damage plants, flowers, or trees.
   • Collect all the litter you see, not just yours.

"God has used rocks in the Bible as symbols of a sacred place. Let's look at this rock formation as sacred, a place to take care of, a place to learn about ourselves, others, and God. We are here to be safe, to trust God, to trust one another, and to have lots of fun.

"We have the opportunity today to push and to support one another. We all have limits; this trip can help you find your limits. Then, in a loving, supporting group, you will have the chance to push past those limits. No one should feel forced or pressured to try anything, and everyone should feel as if she or he can try again. We can refer to this kind of experience as 'Challenge by Choice.'"

SESSION 2

☞ Start by debriefing the day. Invite the group members to tell their stories. Talk about the triumphs over fear, the struggles, the fun.

☞ Ask some of these questions:

- What was hard about climbing (or other activities) today?
- What was easy?
  - What did you like the best?
  - Did you push yourself today?
    - What did you learn about yourself today?
    - What did you learn about someone else?
  - Did you find yourself praying a lot today?

☞ Then ask:

- What are some similarities between climbing and knowing God?
  - What did you learn or observe about climbing and spiritual truths?

☞ Have each person find a partner. The teams are to search for New Testament Scriptures that talk about the element of rock and that indicate the importance of a rock or a foundation. Invite the pairs to tell the group what they found.

☞ End the session by saying something like: "In Luke 37–40 the Bible tells about Jesus' final trip to Jerusalem. As Jesus is approaching the city, the Pharisees tell Jesus to rebuke the disciples for what they are saying about him. Jesus says that if the disciples keep silent, the rocks will sing out in praise. So look around and find ways to praise God. And look for ways that nature praises God."

SATURDAY NIGHT WORSHIP

☞ *Opening:* Begin with a few "rock" songs again.

☞ *Prayer:* Pray for God to be present in this time of worship and thank God for the adventure the group has had today.

☞ *Scripture:* Have one or two persons read aloud Psalm 40:1-3 and Matthew 7:24-27.

☞ *Message:* Say something like: "We live in a world where what is 'in' today may be 'out' tomorrow. Many things in our life may change often: jobs, boyfriends/girlfriends, schools, pop culture. The only constancy in terms of human creation is change. On the other hand, Scripture has remained true and relevant for thousands of years. As Christians it is important to have a firm foundation in the words of Jesus. If we are grounded in Christ, we will be able to endure change. Knowing and following Christ gives us a guide throughout life. God promises wisdom to those who trust in Jesus Christ."

☞ *Closing Songs*

☞ *Closing Prayer:* Ask God to grant rocklike wisdom and guidance.

SUNDAY

SUNDAY WORSHIP

Preparation: If the site for worship has changed, reassemble the rock altar in the new location.

☞ *Scripture:* Begin with someone reading aloud Psalm 62:1-2.

☞ *Prayer:* Pray that God will be part of the worship. Ask for understanding and for God to be at work in each person in the group.

☞ *Songs:* Sing some uplifting ones that your group thoroughly enjoys.

☞ *Scripture:* Have someone read aloud Matthew 16:13-18.

☞ *Message:* Say something like: "Jesus refers to Peter as the rock that the church will be built on. Jesus may have known that Peter would show weakness before he got stronger (Peter later tells three different persons that he doesn't even know Jesus). But Jesus believed that Peter would do great things to build the church once Jesus' earthly mission was over. Not only that, but the disciples and other followers will later look to Peter, the rock, as a leader of this new movement responsible for spreading the gospel.

"While Peter would not shoulder the responsibility all by himself, he would set an example for others to follow. Jesus has told us all what to do; so we too are part of this rock that Jesus is using to build his church. We are charged to go forth and do likewise (Luke 10:37) just as the good Samaritan did. We are charged in the Great Commission (Matthew 28:18-20) to go and make disciples of all nations. These efforts are all part of the rock on which the church is built."

☛ *Rock Review:* Have each person come to the altar and get his or her rock. If anyone cannot remember which one is hers or his, any old rock will do. As the participants come to the front and get a rock, have them tell the group one way they think they can be a rock in their daily life.

☛ *Group Comments:* Once everyone has had a chance to comment (remember the slogan "Challenge by Choice"), make your observations about the rock you brought. Then wrap up the time with a summary of the worship or anything else that comes to mind. Tell the group you will be taking your rock home to put in the youth room or your office as a reminder of the weekend. Have all the participants write their name on the rock.

☛ *Closing Prayer*

Knowing the God of the Edge

WHAT'S THE POINT?

One of the core concepts in Christianity is that everyone can have a personal relationship with God. However, the Bible never mentions the word *relationship* as such. (Keep in mind that early adolescents are just beginning to grasp the notion of having meaningful relationships with *people*.) Yet, the idea of a relationship with God is absolutely central to the Christian faith. This retreat can give youth a chance to understand what it means to have a profound relationship with God.

WHY IT MATTERS

"You are the one who put me together inside my mother's body, / and I praise you because of the wonderful way you created me. / Everything you do is marvelous! / Of this I have no doubt" (Psalm 139:13-14).

OTHER SCRIPTURE REFERENCES IN THIS RETREAT

Genesis 1:26-31
1 Samuel 16:14-23
1 Samuel 18:1-9
1 Samuel 20:12-17
Psalm 139
Matthew 6:19-34
Romans 5:1, 2, 5
Philippians 3:10-14
James 2:20-22
1 John 1:3-6

Retreat Schedule

Friday Night

7:00	Arrive and unpack
7:30	Loopy time
8:00	Expectations
8:15	Break
8:25	Session 1
9:00	Break
9:15	Worship
10:00	Bed prep
10:30	Lights out

Saturday

7:00	Wake up
8:00	Breakfast
8:30	One-on-one time
9:00	Break
10:00	Session 2
11:30	Break
12:00	Lunch
1:00	Free time
3:00	Session 3
4:30	Break
5:00	Vespers
6:00	Dinner
7:00	Free time
8:00	Session 4
9:00	Break
9:30	Worship
10:30	Bed prep
11:00	Lights out

Sunday

6:00	Pack-up and breakfast
6:45	Closing worship
7:00	Depart
	One-on-one time on vans

SESSION 1: WHAT'S A RELATIONSHIP?

The purpose of this session is to define the term *relationship* and understand it as something that is always changing and that requires maintenance.

☛ Open the session with prayer. Ask God to help everyone have a clear understanding of God and of how humans can relate to God.

☛ Discuss these questions:

- What does the word *relationship* mean?
- What do you think of when you hear the word?
- What's the difference between a good relationship and a bad one?

☛ Form teams of four to six persons (if possible, separate by ages; sixth and twelfth graders have vastly different perceptions of relationship issues). Hand out copies of the worksheet "David, the Man of Many Relationships" and have the teams respond to those statements and questions.

☛ Bring everyone back together for a period of discussion. Allow about ten minutes for the different teams to report back. Ask some of these additional questions:

- Name some different types of relationships.
- How does the way you act affect your relationships with others?
- How do your feelings and emotions affect your relationships?
- How do your thoughts affect your relationships?
- How do circumstances affect your relationships?
- Name some other factors that affect your relationships and tell how they affect them.
- Who are you closest to? most distant from? Why?

☛ Close the discussion by saying something like: "Some things we can control in our relationships, and others we cannot. Many factors combine to enhance our relationships or to tear them down. We will spend the weekend together exploring our relationship with God. When we come together for worship, try to think about how God relates to us and how we relate to God."

☛ Close with a prayer.

FRIDAY NIGHT WORSHIP

Preparation: This worship experience will focus on the fact that God makes the first move to be with us. Choose four volunteers for a dramatic reading, with each one reading aloud a portion of Psalm 139:1-18, 23-24. Have the readers station themselves amongst the total group at the appropriate time.

☛ *Opening Prayer:* Thank God for being near and ask for reassurrance of God's presence.

☛ *Scripture:* Read aloud Genesis 1:26-31.

☛ *Song:* Play or sing a song that has to do with creation and beauty or thanksgiving, such as one of these selections:

= "If I Stand"
= "Calling Out Your Name"

☛ *Scripture:* Have the four readers assume their stations and each read aloud his or her section of Psalm 139:1-18, 23-24.

☛ *Song:* Sing or play a song similar to the first one, such as

+ "We Are Grateful"

☛ **Closing Prayer:** Have a few (four or five) persons pray aloud, thanking God for being near and for reaching out to us.

SESSION 2: GOD WANTS TO BE WITH ME?

The purpose of this session is to help the participants understand that we are called into relationship with God.

☛ Ask:

- Do you think that God pursues a relationship with us?
- How do you know, one way or the other?

☛ Conduct a mock debate (allow forty-five minutes). Break into two teams. Have each one take a different side on this statement: GOD SEEKS US OUT FIRST BEFORE WE SEEK GOD (*true* or *false*).

☛ Give the teams twenty minutes to do research and to plan their debate strategy. Hand out copies of the following schedule, or write it where everyone can see it. Emphasize to the youth that they will need to plan for the whole time before the debate starts. Mention these Scripture helps:

- TRUE: Genesis 1:26-31; Psalm 139
- FALSE: James 2:20-22; 1 John 1:3-6

  Debate Schedule

  True Side—opening argument (3 minutes)
  False Side—opening argument (3 minutes)
  True Side—rebuttal (2 minutes)
  False Side—rebuttal (2 minutes)

  Gather thoughts (1 minute)

  False Side—closing statement (3 minutes)
  True Side—closing statement (3 minutes)

☛ Give the debate participants these guidelines:

- During "argument" stages, the opposite team cannot speak. The rebuttal time is designated for making a response.
- Use as much factual information and Scripture as possible.
- Control one's own personal feelings and reactions during the debate.

☛ After the debate, ask each side how it felt to argue their points.

☛ Read aloud 1 John 4:19, then ask:

- How does it feel to know that God seeks us out first?
- Why is God's seeking us important?

SESSION 3: HOW DO WE BUILD A RELATIONSHIP WITH GOD?

The purpose of this session is to explore ways to grow nearer to God and to have a more authentic relationship with God.

☛ Summarize what the group has done so far this weekend. Then say something like: "We can improve our relationships by giving more to them. The way you treat someone can improve your relationship with that person. The same is true for our relationship with God."

☛ Have the youth return to their same teams from Session 1. Give each team a copy of the discussion guide "Knowing God." Allow thirty to forty-five minutes for responding to the questions.

Vespers

☛ *Prayer*

☛ *Songs:* Consider these possible selections:

  + "As Long As You Are Here With Me"
  + "Remember"

☛ *Scripture:* Have someone read aloud Romans 5:1, 2, 5.

☛ *Offering:* Invite the group to write down some words of praise to God.

☛ *Songs:* possible selections:

  + "You Make Your Home in Me"
  + "Mercy Me"

☛ *Closing Prayer*

SESSION 4: PUTTING IT INTO PRACTICE

The purpose of this session is to challenge the participants to practice and apply the relationship skills they have learned thus far.

☛ Open the session by saying: "So we have spent all this time talking about our relationship with God, but we could go home and nothing would be different. When we return to our teams, everyone will have a chance to get personal. I urge you to take advantage of this opportunity and to show respect for others. What can you do right now to enhance your relationship with God?"

☛ Have the youth return to their groups and work through the discussion guide "Growing With God."

☛ Prepare the group members for worship.

SATURDAY NIGHT WORSHIP

☛ *Opening Prayer*

☛ *Scripture:* Read aloud Philippians 3:10-14.

☛ *Song:* Possible selection: = "If I Stand."

☛ *Message:* Challenge the participants to continually renew their relationship with God. Remind the youth of their discussion of attitudes and actions that may improve one's relationship with God.

☛ *Offering:* Have the youth meet in teams and compose a covenant about things the group members can do to help one another with their relationship with God.

☛ *Song:* Play = "Sometimes by Step."

☛ *Closing Prayer*

Worksheet

David, the Man of Many Relationships

Read through 1 Samuel 16:14-23; 18:5-9.

1. Describe the type of relationship that David had with Saul.

2. What situations made their relationship good?

3. What made it bad?

4. What emotions affected their relationship?

5. What behaviors affected their relationship?

Read through 1 Samuel 18:1-4; 20:12-17.

1. Describe the type of relationship David had with Jonathan.

2. What helped to strengthen their relationship?

3. What made their relationship tough to maintain?

4. What types of sacrifices did they have to make to keep a good relationship?

Knowing God

1. What are some ways we can improve our communication with God?

2. When we pray, how much time do we spend focused on God? on ourselves? on others?

3. How have you improved in your prayer life?

4. Do you enjoy reading the Bible? Why or why not?

5. How can you get more meaning out of the Bible when you read?

6. What are some things to look for to help increase your interest?

7. What parts of the Bible have been interesting to you? Why?

8. How can you increase your love for God?

9. How can you respect God more?

10. Why is it sometimes hard to praise God?

Growing With God

(WARNING—high-risk questions!)

1. Describe your relationship with God. How close do you feel to God right now? (Use a line if it helps: I _____ God.)

2. What actions (that you actually do) help keep you close to God?

3. What attitudes do you have that help keep you close to God?

4. What might you be doing that is distancing you from God?

5. What attitudes do you have that are separating you from God?

6. What can you commit to changing (attitudes and actions) that will improve your relationship with God?

7. What can you commit to continuing or adding (attitudes and actions) that will help your relationship with God?

8. What do you think God is doing to get closer to you?

9. What can the group do to help you with your relationship with God?

Roped Up: On God's Team

WHAT'S THE POINT?

Building a sense of family and unity in a group is important. This task may be even more crucial if the group reflects a great deal of diversity. Through Bible study, worship, and a number of fun games, the participants in this retreat will experience one another and develop a bond of respect and joy.

WHY IT MATTERS

"If one part of our body hurts, we hurt all over. If one part of our body is honored, the whole body will be happy"

(1 Corinthians 12:26).

OTHER SCRIPTURE REFERENCES IN THIS RETREAT

1 Corinthians 12:14-27
Philippians 4:4-9
Joshua 2
Matthew 5:3-12

Retreat Schedule

Friday Night

6:00	Arrive and unload
7:00	Meet with group
	—Overview, expectations, and
	—other rules for the weekend
7:30	Loopy time
8:30	Break
9:30	Worship
10:30	Bed prep
11:00	Lights out

Saturday

7:30	Breakfast
9:00	Loopy time
10:00	Session 1
11:00	Break
12:00	Lunch
1:00	Session 2
2:00	Break
2:30	Session 3
3:30	Break
5:30	Dinner
7:30	Loopy time (possible options):
	—games; a songfest around a bonfire
10:00	Break
10:30	Worship
11:30	Bed prep
12:00	Lights out

Sunday

7:30	Breakfast
8:00	Vespers
9:00	Loopy time
10:00	Clean up and pack
11:00	Worship
12:00	Depart

FRIDAY NIGHT

FRIDAY NIGHT WORSHIP: GOD'S TEAM IS A BODY

Preparation: For the skit you will need large pieces of cardboard cut out in the shape of these "characters": a toe, an eye, a pectoral muscle, and a spleen. Have the persons portraying these characters wear the pieces of cardboard around their neck to indicate what part of the body they represent. Also provide a Bible with a bookmark holding the place of 1 Corinthians 12:14-27. Unless every member of your group is an extrovert, choose the cast ahead of time and have them practice.

Cast of "Skippy, the Little Toe":
   Skippy the Toe—a meek little person with low self-esteem
   Iris the Eye—a charming Southern belle
   Franz the Pectoral Muscle—a pumped-up guy with a pumped-up ego
   Mr. Kranz the Spleen—a crabby old man

The main character, Skippy, is a little toe, who feels worthless and believes that a little toe has no real function. The other characters try to help Skippy realize that he is an important part of the body; but they are so focused on how important they are that they only make Skippy feel worse. In the middle of his depression, Skippy picks up the Bible and reads 1 Corinthians 12:14-27.

☛ *Call the group to worship* by singing a few songs that will put them in a worshipful mood. Here are some suggestions:

   + "Jesus Is the Rock"
   + "We Are Grateful"
   + "Lean On"

☛ *Opening Prayer:* Ask God to show your group how to be the body of Christ.

☛ *Skit:* Have the cast present "Skippy, the Little Toe."

☛ *Message:* After the presentation, say: "Each of us is a part of the body of Christ. Ask yourself tonight: What are my talents and how can I use them to be a part of God's team?"

☛ *Closing Prayer:* Ask God to help each participant use his or her talents to be a contributing member of God's team.

NOTE: The three sessions of this retreat are intended to be conducted in small groups of ten to twelve. If your group is larger, do this work in smaller teams with team leaders who are familiar with the activities in the sessions.

SATURDAY

SESSION 1: A PEACE OF GOD'S TEAM

Supply paper grocery bags, pens or pencils, slips of paper, markers.

☛ Open the session with prayer.

☛ Read aloud Philippians 4:4-9.

☛ Ask the group:

   • Is it possible to do the things God asks in this passage, or is God asking the impossible?
   • Why would God tell us to do these things?

☛ Distribute the paper grocery bags, and have each participant write the Scripture verses from Philippians on one side of her or his bag. On the other side the youth are to draw themselves or list some qualities they would like others to see in them. Hand out slips of paper and have the youth write down things that keep them from becoming the person they want to be. The group members are to crumple their slips of paper and throw them in the bags. Then allow volunteers to tell what they wrote.

☛ Have someone again read aloud Philippians 4:6-7. Point out that the peace of God comes when we give away all the "trash" in our life to Christ in prayer.

☛ Pray silently for the concerns in the bags. Then have someone voice a prayer thanking God for taking out our "trash."

☛ Sing + "Jesus Is the Rock."

SESSION 2: GOD CAN USE ANYONE

☞ Ask for several volunteers to read aloud Joshua 2, or have the whole group partici-pate (each person may read aloud two or three verses).

☞ If your group is large, form two or three smaller teams. Have each team pre-pare a skit based on Joshua 2. If you wish, have the teams adapt the Scripture to modern times or give it a futuristic setting. The idea is for the group mem-bers to have fun with this activity.

☞ Invite the teams to perform their skits for one another.

☞ Ask:

- Who took risks in this story?
- Why does God sometimes ask us to take risks?
- What are some risks God might be asking you to take?

☞ Point out that God can use anybody who is will-ing to be a servant and to take some risks.

SESSION 3: AS MESSY AS YOU WANT TO BE

☞ Select one or more of the games on pages 76–80 (possible suggestions: "High-Water Mark," "Cold Feet," or "Make Me Smile"). Although some of these games are competitive, they can still fit the purpose of Session 3, which is to provide a fun experience for the participants. Such experiences are part of developing a bond of joy.

☞ If you wish, have a campfire and songfest after the games.

SATURDAY NIGHT WORSHIP: PART OF GOD'S TEAM

☛ *Opening Prayer:* Ask God to be with the group in worship and to help everyone understand what it takes to live a Christian life.

☛ *Scripture:* Ask someone to read aloud Matthew 5:3-12. As each beatitude is read, have two persons pantomime it for the rest of the group. (Example: "Blessed are those who mourn, for they will be comforted"—One person silently sobs as the other person comforts her or him.)

☛ *Songs:* Sing these or other selections:

  + "We Are Grateful"
  + "Mercy Me"
  + "You Make Your Home in Me"

☛ *Message*: Ask:

  • What do you see as the characteristics of a good Christian?
  • What qualities does the Scripture we just read identify as the characteristics of a good Christian?
  • Which characteristics are your strongest?
  • Which ones are your weakest?

☛ Challenge the group members to continue trying to develop their strengths and overcome their weaknesses.

☛ *Closing Prayer:* Praise God for giving us both strengths and weaknesses to develop and modify.

SUNDAY

SUNDAY MORNING VESPERS

☛ *Songs:* Sing any that have become group favorites over the weekend.

☛ *Opening Prayer:* Thank God for being a part of the weekend and for sending Christ to model the way to live as a part of the body of Christ.

☛ *Scripture:* Have two different youth read aloud 1 Corinthians 12:14-27 and Matthew 5:3-12.

☛ *Optional Responses:* Give the participants a chance to tell about any changes they plan to make as a result of this retreat. Challenge the group members to continue thinking of themselves as a body and working hard to treat one another with love.

☛ *Closing Prayer:* Thank God for the weekend and ask for help in living together in unity.

☛ *Sing* + "Take My Hand" as a benediction.

Tied Together: Relating to *Others*

WHAT'S THE POINT?

This retreat focuses on skills that can help Christian youth have deeper, more fulfilling relationships. Our life is not lived in isolation; and for each person we encounter on a regular basis, there is a relationship that can benefit by care and attention. Through proper maintenance of our relationships, other people become significant parts of our lives.

WHY IT MATTERS

"If you love each other, everyone will know that you are my disciples" (John 13:35).

OTHER SCRIPTURE REFERENCES IN THIS RETREAT

1 Samuel 20:42
Matthew 7:12
Ecclesiastes 4:9-12
Romans 12:19-16

Retreat Schedule

Friday Night

6:00	Arrive and unload
7:00	Meet with group
	—Overview of weekend
	—Expectations of youth and leaders
	—Other rules for the weekend
7:30	Loopy time
8:30	Break
9:30	Worship
10:30	Bed prep
11:00	Lights out

Saturday

7:30	Breakfast
	—One-on-time immediately following
9:00	Loopy time
10:00	Session 1
11:30	Break
12:00	Lunch
1:00	Session 2
2:30	Free time
5:30	Dinner
6:30	Session 3
8:00	Loopy time
	—possibly a campfire, video, or game
10:00	Break
10:30	Worship
11:30	Bed prep
12:00	Lights out

Sunday

7:30	Breakfast
	—One-on-time immediately following
9:00	Loopy time
9:30	Worship
10:00	Clean up and pack
11:00	Depart

FRIDAY NIGHT

FRIDAY NIGHT WORSHIP: SEEING GOD IN OUR RELATIONSHIPS WITH OTHERS

Preparation: Provide a large sheet of paper and crayons or markers. Draw a cross in the middle of the paper, leaving plenty of writing and drawing space around the cross. Hang the sheet on the wall (but not too high; the participants will be writing on it later in the worship service). If you wish, light candles to help transform the meeting room into a place of worship.

☛ *Songs:* Begin by singing songs that the group enjoys. Consider these selections:

+ "Mercy Me"
+ "Take My Hand"
+ "Jesus Is the Rock"

☛ *Opening Prayer:* Invite someone to pray aloud, thanking God for the relationships that make our lives more meaningful.

☛ *Scripture:* Give some background information before you read aloud 1 Samuel 20:42. Say something like: "David was good friends with Jonathan, King Saul's son. When Saul became jealous of David's popularity, he tried to kill David, forcing him to flee into the desert." Then read the Bible verse.

☛ *Message:* Say something like: "In this Scripture verse we see an example of an extraordinary relationship between two persons. David and Jonathan made a commitment not only to each other, but also to God. Just as God was an active part of David and Jonathan's relationship, so also can God be a part of our relationships."

☛ *Offering:* Say something like: "Think of one relationship (with parents, a friend, or others) that you want to dedicate to God. After you have chosen a relationship, draw a picture (on the sheet of paper with the cross) that symbolizes the relationship you want to dedicate to God. These symbols will serve as a reminder to us throughout the weekend."

☛ *Closing Prayer:* Offer a prayer of thanks to God for human relationships.

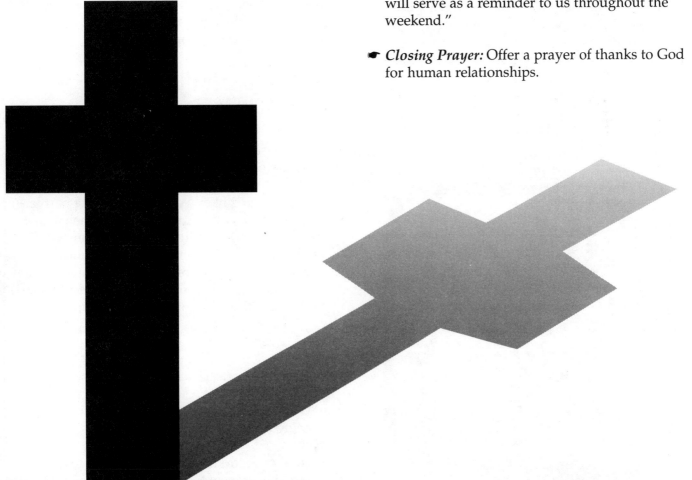

SATURDAY

SESSION 1: OUR EMOTIONAL BANK ACCOUNT

(This concept is described in *The Seven Habits of Highly Effective People*, by Stephen R. Covey [Simon and Schuster, 1989].)

☛ Let the discussion in this session develop naturally without feeling a need to stick strictly to the suggested questions. Also, feel free to include any personal experiences that will make the points more real.

☛ Say something like: "Some say we have emotional bank accounts, just as there are financial bank accounts that involve deposits and withdrawals."

☛ Ask:

• What might be some examples of deposits one could make in someone else's emotional bank account? (kindness, honesty, empathy, loyalty)
• What might be examples of emotional withdrawals? (disrespect, neglect, betrayal of trust, over-reacting)
• What do you think might happen in a relationship if withdrawals exceed deposits in one's personal emotional account and it becomes overdrawn? (The trust level is low; meaningful communication is a rarity.)

☛ Then say: "One writer suggests these major deposits we can make in others' emotional bank accounts:

a. Understand the person.
b. Remember the little things.
c. Honor commitments.
d. Show personal integrity.
e. Apologize sincerely for an emotional withdrawal."

☛ Read aloud Matthew 7:12, then ask:

• How does this Scripture apply to understanding others?
• When has someone showed you a small act of kindness that meant a lot to you?
• When has a broken promise caused a major withdrawal from your emotional bank account?
• Why is it important not to wait to apologize when we realize that we have done something wrong?

☛ Have the participants form two or three teams. Invite each team to create a skit based on the idea of the emotional bank account. Give the youth the freedom to be as creative and off-the-wall as they want to be. When the teams are ready, have them make their presentations.

SESSION 2: A PARTNERSHIP OF PERCENTAGES

Props: a plastic grocery bag (or other bag) with handles; pieces of thread.

☛ Say something like: "A relationship is a partnership between two or more persons. The partners must take responsibility for the relationship. We tend to think of the persons in a relationship dividing the responsibility equally between them. In actuality, each person should assume responsibility for 100 percent of the relationship."

☛ Play "Everybody Up" (see page 76).

☛ Read aloud Ecclesiastes 4:9-12, then ask:

• What do these verses say about the benefits of being part of a relationship?

• How can working as a team lead to greater accomplishment?

- How can you help friends if they "fall" as in verse 10?

☞ Say something like: "Think of a cord made up of three separate strands. Each strand gives 100 percent of its being to the total strength of the rope. Then imagine removing a few fibers from each strand and then attaching a load to the cord. Because the individual strands are no longer contributing 100 percent to the rope, its strength will be diminished."

☞ To further illustrate this point, invite each person to find a small rock outdoors to bring back to the group. Each participant is to place his or her rock in a plastic grocery bag or another bag with handles. Now pass out a piece of thread about one foot long to each person. Ask for a few volunteers to try to lift the bag one by one by placing their thread through the handles and lifting on the ends of the thread. The individual threads will invariably break (if you have a small group you may need to add some stones to the bag or find some bigger rocks). After a few unsuccessful attempts to lift the bag with one piece of thread, try two or three. After these fail (make sure the bag is heavy enough that these do fail), collect the strings from the rest of the group and use all of them to lift the bag.

☞ Ask:
- How might you make sure that you are giving 100 percent?

☞ Make a list on a large sheet of paper of examples of positive things the group members have seen and done in their own relationships.

☞ Have the youth form teams of three or four. Assign each team one of the following passages to study (the members are to identify what the passage teaches us about relating to others):
- Ruth 1:16
- 1 Samuel 20:41-42
- Matthew 22:37-40
- John 15:13
- Acts 4:32
- Romans 12:9-16
- 1 Corinthians 13

☞ Have the teams report back to the larger group. Then close the session with prayer.

SESSION 3: THE LOST ARTS OF AMERICA

☞ Say something like: "Our relationships involve two basic and essential 'lost arts': listening and asking good questions. This session will look at how we can use these lost arts to improve our relationships with others."

☞ Take two or three volunteers to another room and explain that they will go before the group to answer questions about their favorite hobby (a sport, reading, or whatever). As the volunteers are getting their instructions, another leader should direct the other group members to ask questions related to any commonplace activity (washing a car, washing one's hair, painting, and so on). So someone might ask the volunteers, "How often do you do this activity?" or "What do you do if it rains?"

☞ After several minutes of questioning, explain that the point of this game was to demonstrate the importance of clarity in communication.

☞ Say something like: "Let's consider then, the skills of listening and asking good questions."

☞ (Much of the following information is based on "Habit 5"—Seek First to Understand, Then to Be Understood" as described in Stephen R. Covey's *The Seven Habits of Highly Effective People*. Paraphrase it as you see fit.)

I. *Listening.* Of four forms of basic communication—reading, writing, speaking, and listening—we probably receive the least amount of formal training in listening. However, we probably use this form more than the other three. To practice good listening we must do three things:

   A. *listen with our ears.* To show we are listening, we can respond by
      1. repeating what we hear;
      2. using our own words to paraphrase what we hear.

   B. *listen with our eyes.*
      1. Body language makes up a large part of communication.
      2. Speakers use their hands to emphasize or explain information.

3. Speakers show emotions through facial expressions and posture.

C. *listen with our heart.*
   1. We are to try to hear what is behind what we hear.
   2. We try to feel what another person is feeling in order to better understand him or her.
   3. We resist our natural tendency to interpret things from our own point of view and instead see the world through the eyes of the person we are listening to.
   4. We combine logic and intuition, to transform simple hearing and seeing into good, effective listening.

II. *Asking Good Questions.* Here are guidelines for good questions:

   A. A good question is relevant.

   B. A good question demonstrates understanding that we already possess.

   C. A good question seeks to gain needed understanding.

☞ Next, play a game of "corporate espionage." This game will give the group members a chance to practice some of the communication skills they just considered as they attempt to copy your "high-tech" product.

Preparation: Create an original model of a "product," using any materials you have readily available. The product could be anything from a "space modulator" to a "human/cyborg relations protocol droid." Use paper cups, straws, toothpicks, tape, or anything you want; the more complex the creation the better. Set up your creation somewhere out of sight. Gather enough sets of similar materials for every six people in your group. Feel free to include in the sets extra stuff that is not needed. While the sets don't have to be identical, each one should contain the materials needed to build an exact replica of your product.

☞ Form teams of roughly six people. Give each team a set of materials. Each team is to pick one person to be their spy (oops—product research engineer) and one person to be the spy's contact. The rest of the team members are the engineers responsible for copying the product. At no time may the spy or the contact handle any of the materials used in the product's construction. The spies will be the only persons in the group to see the original creation. Their job is to describe to their contact how to build the product. The contact then goes back to the production engineers and tells them how to put together the product. The spy and the contact should meet in a place where the spy cannot see what the engineers are building and the contact cannot see the original product. The following rules will govern the type of communication that takes place between the spy, the contact, and the engineers:

For *Phase 1* of the game (about ten minutes), the spy may describe to the contact how to build the product. The spy is to use only verbal communication (no hand motions or gestures); the contact may not ask any questions. The contact must simply relay the information from the spy to the engineers.

In *Phase 2* (about five minutes), there can be both verbal and visual communication between the spy and the contact. The contact may ask as many questions as she or he likes.

Phase 3 should last only about two minutes. At this point allow both the contact and the spy to see the original product and allow both of them to see the product their engineers are working on. Both the spy and the contact can tell the engineers how to re-create the product; but as in Phase 1, they may use only verbal communication. Remember that the engineers are the only ones allowed to handle the building materials.

☛ Spend some time debriefing by talking about how the groups were able to practice the "lost arts." Some possible questions to ask:

- How well did you listen to one another?
- How did being able to ask questions help your group?
- What was helpful about using more than just verbal communication?
- Was it helpful for the spy to be able to see what the group was building? Why?
- What are some things your group did well?
- Did you discover that certain communication skills need work? If so, what do you want to improve?

SATURDAY NIGHT WORSHIP

Preparation: This worship activity will work best indoors, especially on a concrete or tile floor. Provide eight plastic cups (the sixteen-ounce ones work fine). You will also need a lot of poker chips. The skit will take place from stage left to stage right. On the right place a cross and many candles (the candles could be your only light source). Have about six volunteers practice the following skit:

The main character, Chip, starts his day with cup in hand. Chip encounters Mom, who is holding a cup of chips. Mom makes positive comments to Chip such as: "Have a great day at school, Chip." "From all the studying you did, I know you will do well on your test." "I made you some breakfast." While she is interacting with Chip, she takes a few chips from her cup and puts them in his. Chip makes a few responses (whatever comes naturally).

Mom leaves. Chip finds himself at school. Beth is a self-centered friend who always takes instead of gives. She starts talking about herself. She tells how much trouble she is in at home. She tells how she lost her boyfriend. While she talks, Beth is taking chips out of Chip's cup. Chip also gives some as he tries to build her up. The bell rings and they split up.

Beth leaves and Chip meets up with Coach. Coach is mad at Chip for being a slacker. According to him, Chip's latest game performance was the worst he has ever seen. Coach demands that Chip be the first at practice today to get in some extra laps. (*Many chips are taken from Chip's cup.*)

Coach leaves and Dave comes in. As Dave comments on how Chip is looking glum, he puts in some chips. He asks how things are going and offers to help in any way he can, all the while putting chips in Chip's cup. Chip tells Dave about the test coming up next hour, about Beth, and about Coach. Chip adds to Dave's cup while commenting that Dave is always interested in other people, and is a good friend.

Chip has now made it to the cross. Chip kneels at the cross and starts talking about the good points and the bad points of his day—what took from him and what gave him joy. Chip tells God that he is tired and that his cup is empty. Chip asks to be filled again. At that time "God" comes over with two cups completely full of chips. "God" slowly pours the contents of both cups into Chip's cup.

☛ *Music:* Set a worshipful mood. Someone could sing a solo or play a guitar. Or use some instrumental music. Have the total group enter the place of worship while the music is playing and the candles are burning at the cross.

☛ *Scripture:* Read aloud Matthew 7:7 and Mark 12:30-31, then present the skit.

☛ *Message:* After the skit say something like: "In every life, with every person, we have the power to add, or to take away. In dealing with others, we can either build or destroy. Language, attitude, taking, giving, listening, smiling—all make an impact on the people around us. When we choose to have a positive impact, we have access to all of God's resources.

"Through prayer, we can get our own cup refilled. But a cup can hold only so much. If it is full, you cannot handle anything more. But if you use what you have, God will fill you up again. God may use the Bible, other people, a sermon, or prayer to refill your cup. As you leave here, think about how you interact with people. Do you just take what you want, or do you ask for help? Do you offer help, or just walk on by? Are you getting involved in people's lives? Do you build up, or take away? Are you hurting others, or helping them to heal?"

SUNDAY

SUNDAY MORNING WORSHIP

If the weather permits, select an outside spot for this worship segment.

☞ *Songs:* Begin with selections such as these:

  = "Sometimes by Step"
  + "We Are Grateful"

☞ *Opening Prayer:* Pray that God will join the group in worship and that God's Spirit will open the heart of everyone present.

☞ *Scripture:* Have someone read aloud Romans 12:9-16.

☞ *Optional Responses:* Invite volunteers in the group to stand and answer:

- Will you view your relationships differently after this weekend? If so, in what ways?
- What are you going to do differently in your relationship with your parents? your friends? your siblings?
- How is your relationship with God going to be different?

☞ *Songs:* Sing upbeat praise songs, such as + "Jesus Is the Rock."

☞ *Closing Prayer:* Thank God for all the relationships in our life.

Camped Out: Basic Christian Beliefs

WHAT'S THE POINT?

This retreat will help youth examine the basic beliefs of Christians. The group will explore what it means to believe in Christ and uncover the fundamental tenets of the faith. This experience will be meaningful for those who are new to the church as well as "veterans" searching for their roots.

WHY IT MATTERS

"God loved the people of this world so much that he gave his only Son, so that everyone who has faith in him will have eternal life and never really die. God did not send his Son into the world to condemn its people. He sent him to save them!" (John 3:16-17).

OTHER SCRIPTURE REFERENCES IN THIS RETREAT

Genesis 1:1	John 3:16
Matthew 1:18	John 6:47
Matthew 27:24	John 11:25
Mark 16:19	Acts 2:4
Luke 22:19-20	Romans 12:5
Luke 23: 33, 46, 53	1 Timothy 4:1
Luke 24:6	1 John 1:9

Retreat Schedule

Friday

6:00	Arrive and unload
7:00	Meet with group
	—Retreat overview
	—Expectations of youth and leaders
	—Other rules of the weekend
7:30	Session 1
8:30	Loopy time/Break
9:30	Worship
10:30	Bed prep
11:00	Lights out

Saturday

7:00	Wake up
7:30	Breakfast
9:00	Loopy time
10:00	Session 2
11:30	Break
12:00	Lunch
1:00	Session 3
3:00	Free time
5:30	Dinner/free time
7:30	Loopy time/songs
10:00	Break
10:30	Worship
11:00	Bed prep
11:30	Lights out

Sunday

7:00	Wake up
7:30	Breakfast
9:00	Loopy time
10:00	Clean up/pack/free time
11:00	Closing worship

SESSION 1: BASE CAMP

Preparation: Make a copy of the Apostles' Creed (page 45) for each member of the group.

☛ Say something like: "Suppose you are part of a team that has discovered the cure for a major disease. As you start to tell the world about your discovery, each person on your team tells a different story about how people can get cured. Some of the versions are so inaccurate that some people with the disease actually get worse after following those instructions. You and your group come together to agree on the essential truth about how people can be cured. The story you come up with together would serve a purpose similar to that of the Apostles' Creed. Early in church history, believers felt a need to agree on what a person should believe to be called a Christian."

☛ Hand out copies of the creed and have everyone read it in unison.

☛ Have the group members form pairs and give each pair one of the Scriptures listed below. Each small team is to look up the Bible passage and determine which line or lines of the Apostles' Creed correspond to the passage. (If necessary, assign more than one passage to each team.) As each pair reports back to the group, invite everyone else to write the Bible references (book, chapter, and verse) opposite the appropriate lines of the creed. Then have the entire group recite the Apostles' Creed together again.

THE APOSTLES' CREED, ECUMENICAL VERSION

I believe in God, the Father Almighty,	Matthew 6:9
creator of heaven and earth.	Genesis 1:1
I believe in Jesus Christ, his only Son, our Lord,	John 3:16
who was conceived by the Holy Spirit,	Matthew 1:18
born of the Virgin Mary,	Matthew 1:18
suffered under Pontius Pilate,	Matthew 27:24
was crucified, died, and was buried;	Luke 23:33, 46, 53
he descended to the dead.	
On the third day he rose again;	Luke 24:6
he ascended into heaven,	Mark 16:19
is seated at the right hand of the Father,	Mark 16:19
and will come again to judge the living and the dead.	Timothy 4:1
I believe in the Holy Spirit,	Acts: 2:4
the holy catholic church,	Romans 12:5
the communion of saints,	Luke 22:19-20
the forgiveness of sins,	1 John 1:9
the resurrection of the body	John 11:25,
and the life everlasting. Amen.	John 6:47

FRIDAY NIGHT WORSHIP

Preparation: Choose several volunteers to read aloud the Lord's Prayer.

☛ *Play or sing* + "Jesus Is the Rock" or = "Creed."

☛ *Prayer:* Have the volunteers take turns reading aloud the Lord's Prayer.

☛ *Scripture:* Invite someone to read aloud Luke 11:1-13.

☛ *Message:* Say: "The question the disciples asked was, How do we pray? Jesus' response told them what to believe and how to live as well as how to pray. The answer also points to God's grace, to the fact that God's power and presence are available to anyone who asks. These teachings of Jesus' are the cornerstone of the Gospels."

☛ *Closing Song:* Sing + "Lean On."

SATURDAY

SESSION 2: THE ROCK

☛ Say something like: "Christians believe that Jesus Christ is our foundation. But we have different ideas about what that means."

☛ Have two persons read aloud Luke 6:46-49 and 1 Corinthians 3:10-15.

☛ Ask:

- What are some things that could be considered a weak foundation?
- What is the firm foundation talked about in these two Scriptures?
- How can being grounded in Christ help us endure life's hardships?
- How can we build lasting structures on our foundation?

☛ Have another volunteer read aloud Colossians 2:6-7.

☛ Give each person a piece of paper, an envelope, and a pen or pencil. Have the group members write a letter to themselves as a reminder of how they plan to build on the foundation of knowing Christ. The letters should answer the question, What are you going to do to show Jesus Christ's influence and direction in your life? The youth are to address the envelope to themselves and seal the letter inside. Collect the letters. Tell the youth that you will mail the letters back to them at a later date.

SESSION 3: FRUITS OF THE SPIRIT

☛ Form teams of three or four. Give half the teams the "bearing fruit" Bible verses and questions. Give the other teams the "fruit of the Spirit" verses and questions. (We recommend that you use the New Revised Standard Version of the Bible or the New International Version for this activity.) Have each team discuss the Scripture with the help of the suggested questions.

Bearing Fruit: John 15:1-15

- What does it mean to bear fruit?
- What happens to the branches that do not bear fruit?
- What happens to the branches that do bear fruit?
- Can we bear fruit by ourselves? What must we do to bear spiritual fruit?

Fruit of the Spirit: Galatians 5:22-26; 1 Corinthians 13:13

- Briefly describe each "fruit"; give an example and tell why that quality is important.
- What are these spiritual qualities meant to replace in our life?
- Which is the greatest of the qualities? Why?

☛ Call the teams together and ask each one to tell something they learned.

SATURDAY NIGHT WORSHIP:
THE GREAT COMMANDMENT

☞ *Sing* one or more of these selections:

+ "Jesus Is the Rock"
+ "We Are Grateful"
+ "Mercy Me"

☞ *Opening Prayer:* Ask God to be present in this time of worship.

☞ *Message:* Say something like: "When Jesus was asked what is most important for his followers to do, he said 'love.' When Paul was asked what the greatest gift was, he said 'love.' Then he defined love."

☞ Read aloud 1 Corinthians 13:1-13. Then say: "I'm going to read part of this again. This time whenever you hear the word *love*, go up to someone and hold or shake her or his hand or give the person a hug. When you hear *love* again, go to another person." Read aloud 1 Corinthians 13:4-8, 13.

☞ *Closing Prayer:* Thank God for loving us.

SUNDAY

SUNDAY WORSHIP:
THE GREAT COMMISSION

☞ *Sing* + "John 12:26" as an opening prayer.

☞ *Scripture:* Read aloud Matthew 28:18-20.

☞ *Message:* Say something like: "When Jesus calls the first disciples, one of the first things he tells them is the same as one of the last things he will tell them. He tells them that they are called to know him and to bring others to him. We refer to Jesus' last words as the Great Commission. He tells his disciples to go into the world and to teach others to obey the things he has taught them. Now Jesus calls us to do the same. We go back to our homes and schools and friends to tell people what God has done for us and what God can do for them."

☞ *Prayer:* Thank God for everything the group has learned this weekend. Ask God for the strength and courage to share these learnings with others.

☞ *Sing* + "Take My Hand."

NOTE: Decide now when you will mail the letters the youth wrote to themselves. Choose a date that allows enough time to pass so that most of the participants will likely have forgotten the exact wording of their letter.

THE APOSTLES' CREED, ECUMENICAL VERSION

I believe in God, the Father Almighty, _____
creator of heaven and earth. _____

I believe in Jesus Christ, his only Son, our Lord
_____
who was conceived by the Holy Spirit,
_____
born of the Virgin Mary, _____
suffered under Pontius Pilate, _____
was crucified, died, and was buried;
_____
he descended to the dead.
On the third day he rose again; _____
he ascended into heaven, _____
is seated at the right hand of the Father,
_____
and will come again to judge the living and the
dead. _____
I believe in the Holy Spirit, _____
the holy catholic church, _____
the communion of saints, _____
the forgiveness of sins, _____
the resurrection of the body, _____
and the life everlasting. Amen. _____

THE LORD'S PRAYER (ECUMENICAL TEXT)

Our Father in heaven,
    hallowed be your name,
    your kingdom come,
    your will be done, on earth as in heaven.
Give us today our daily bread.
Forgive us our sins
    as we forgive those who sin against us.
Save us from the time of trial
    and deliver us from evil.
For the kingdom, the power, and the glory are yours
    now and for ever. Amen.

Faith From the EDGE

WHAT'S THE POINT?

This retreat deals with four Bible stories in which the main character had to trust God in order to make it through a hard time. Thus we see the importance of maintaining one's faith in God. The intention of this retreat is to inspire youth to test their faith by taking it to the edge.

WHY IT MATTERS

"Faith makes us sure of what we hope for and gives us proof of what we cannot see" (Hebrews 11:1).

OTHER SCRIPTURE REFERENCES IN THIS RETREAT

Genesis 22:1-13
the Book of Job
Matthew 26:17-56

Retreat Schedule

Friday Night

6:00	Arrive and unload
7:00	Meet with group
	—Outline of the retreat
	—Expectations of youth and leaders
7:30	Loopy time
8:30	Break
9:30	Worship
10:30	Bed prep
11:00	Lights out

Saturday

7:00	Wake up
7:30	Breakfast/one-on-one time
9:00	Loopy time
10:00	Session 1
11:30	Break
12:00	Lunch
1:00	Session 2
3:00	Free time
5:30	Dinner/free time
7:30	Loopy time (suggestions):
	—Songfest
	—Beverages and snacks
	—Movie video
	—Adventure game
10:00	Break (get ready for worship)
10:30	Worship
11:00	Bed prep
11:30	Lights out

Sunday

7:00	Wake up
7:30	Breakfast/one-on-one time
9:00	Loopy time
10:00	Clean up/pack/free time
11:00	Closing worship

FRIDAY NIGHT

FRIDAY NIGHT WORSHIP:
ABRAHAM ON THE EDGE

☞ *Set the tone for worship* by playing or singing several songs, such as

= "Awesome God"
= "Sometimes by Step"

☞ *Prayer:* Give thanks to God for letting the group spend time in worship. Ask God to use the worship experience to provide all the participants with spiritual insights.

☞ *Scripture:* Have someone read aloud Genesis 22:1-13.

☞ *Message:* Say something like: "Abraham lived out his faith. He trusted that God was in control. Even though he may not have understood what God was doing in his life, he obeyed. Obedience is often difficult; but as we gain experience with God's direction in our life, it gets easier to let go of our will and let God lead us. Once Abraham knew his task, he carried it out; he did not hesitate to follow through. Abraham's experiences with God led him to trust God. Our experiences will also show God to be trustworthy. Even though we may encounter rough times, God will not give us more than we can handle. The good news is that God is with us throughout our life."

☞ *Scripture:* Have someone read aloud Genesis 22:14-19.

☞ *Closing Prayer:* Before ending with prayer, mention any necessary instructions for the rest of the night. Then say something like: "Tomorrow we will be spending some time learning other stories of faith." Then thank God for being with the group during this period of worship. Give praise for all that the Spirit does for the youth and the leaders.

SATURDAY

SESSION 1: JOB ON THE EDGE

Preparation: Be sure that you have an adequate understanding of the story of Job. The revised Student Bible (New Revised Standard Version) includes some helpful insights and notes. Make separate copies of the four different sections of the "Group Study" sheet (page 50). (If you need to form more than four teams, more than one group will study the same Scripture segment.)

☞ Start with a game (suggested option: "Whose Shoes?" [page 77]).

☞ Form four small teams (no team should have more than eight persons). If necessary, form additional teams. Distribute the "Group Study" sheets, assigning each team a different section of Job's story. Have the youth look at what the Scripture says, why it is said, how it is said. Have the team members answer the questions that are printed on their sheet (the blank portion of the sheet can be used for notes). Then invite each team to tell the total group their findings. After the presentations, talk more about Job's story: Ask:

• How is Job's experience like what we sometimes go through?
• Do you have friends who treat you like Job's friends treated him?

☞ Have someone read aloud Job 42:10-17.

☞ Say something like: "God was with Job throughout his ordeal. Even though Job complained and even cursed the day he was born, he never gave up on God. God seemed to trust that Job would stand firm throughout the devil's testing of him. Job found himself on the physical, emotional, and spiritual edge. How can we draw strength from the story of Job? The main thing to keep in mind is that God is with us always, in both bad times and good times. When we experience family conflicts, personal struggles, or when things look hopeless, God is there. God is also there when things are going smoothly."

SESSION 2: OTHERS ON THE EDGE

☛ Invite the youth to conduct their own search for faith stories. Have the participants gather in teams of about three to six persons. Give each team a blank sheet of paper for recording answers to the questions below. Each team is to look in the Bible for three or four stories of persons whose lives were on the edge. The examples might describe someone's faith being tested or a faith that rings true. When everyone is ready, have each team report their findings to the larger group.

- Who is the main character?
- What is the challenge?
- How does the person meet that challenge?
- How is faith in God expressed or broken?

☛ Invite each team to present a skit about faith. The youth might choose one of their biblical situations to act out or they could make up a contemporary situation of tested faith. Allow adequate writing and rehearsal time. These skits can be performed either during this session or at a campfire Saturday night. The skits can be a fun activity as well as an effective dramatization of a profound topic. Mention to the teams that they have the option of concluding their presentations with an appropriate prayer.

SATURDAY NIGHT WORSHIP: JESUS ON THE EDGE

Preparation: Invite several group members to prepare a presentation of Jesus in his last hours before his crucifixion (see Matthew 26:17-56). They may act out, read about, or sing about the night when Jesus was handed over. The *Jesus Christ Superstar* and/or *Godspell* soundtracks are possible sources for songs dealing with this topic. If you wish, suggest a combination of styles and mediums. The final format of the presentation depends on the location, time, resources, and group talents that are available.

☛ *Prayer:* Ask God to be with the group members as they worship. Pray for understanding and guidance.

☛ *Presentation:* Have the players present the last days of Jesus.

☛ *Message:* Say something like: "Here we see Jesus on the edge. Time was coming to an end for Jesus here on earth. He knew what was coming and he agonized over it. Jesus knew the plan, but he also needed help to go through with it. He went to God in prayer, asking God to find another way to save God's people, which includes all of us. (How many times do we ask God to get us out of something?) But in the end Jesus followed God even unto death. Because of what Jesus did we can draw strength from him, even in our most difficult of times. We can do what we know to be God's will. Even if we find ourselves on the edge of our faith and understanding, we can still stay strong, still be true to God. And because of Jesus' sacrifice, when we do fall short, God is ready to take us back and forgive us."

☛ *Reflection:* Have the group members sit quietly and think about these questions:

- How have you been tempted in the past?
- How have you fallen short?
- When have you held firmly to your beliefs?
- How can you draw strength from Jesus in your everyday life?

☛ *Closing Prayer:* Have each person find a partner. Invite the partners to pray with each other, for each other, and for the group.

SUNDAY WORSHIP: CHOICES AND YOU

Preparation: This worship segment focuses on the subject of choice. Try to find a story about choice to read aloud, such as "The Choice," by Max Lucado, from *In the Eye of the Storm* (Word Publishing, 1994). Or write a story from your own experience and tell it during worship.

☛ *Songs:* Begin worship with some of your group's favorite songs (possible titles):

+ "As Long As You Are Here With Me"
+ "Lean On"
+ "Jesus Is the Rock"

☛ *Prayer:* Thank God for the freedom we have to choose to follow the gospel. Ask the Holy Spirit to be with the youth each time they need to stand up for the sake of the Kingdom, each time their faith is tested.

☛ *Read or tell your story* about choice.

☛ *Message:* Process the story about choice by asking these questions:

• What happened in the story?
• What made it a story about choice?
• What might have happened had the choice been different?

Then say something like: "Choices are a daily and ongoing part of life—what to wear, what to eat, what to do for fun or work, who our friends are, what classes to take. Some of our decisions and actions reflect our basic beliefs. For instance, Do you reach out to friends and family members when they have a problem? Do you sit next to the new person at school or at church?"

☛ *Invitation:* Say: "Today you have the opportunity to make a decision about the rest of your life. Many of our choices involve opportunities to follow Jesus Christ. When you choose to follow Christ, that decision affects all your other decisions. You may have already made that decision or you may want to accept God's call for the first time today. Be sure to tell someone else if you are making such a decision for the first time today."

☛ *Offering:* Give each person an envelope, a pen, and paper. Invite the group members to write a letter to themselves. Ask them to write
• something they learned this weekend
• something they want to stop in their life
• something they wish to start in their life

Have the youth seal their letter in the envelope and write their name and address on the outside. Then ask them to find a partner. Have the partners tell each other something they learned this weekend. If the partners feel comfortable doing so, they may exchange answers to the other two questions. The participants may keep their letter to open at a later time or give it to their partner to mail to them.

☛ *Close with a group prayer.*

Group Study

Background: Job 1 and 2

Your team starts Job's story. What do all the other group members need to know in the way of background on Job? Who are the important characters in this story and why?

Job's friends react: Job 2:11-13; 4:2-11; 5:8-27; 8; 15:1-15; 19

Job was a wealthy community leader. Many people knew Job. He had several good friends, three of whom came to be by his side. What happened next? What did they say to Job? Did they help or hurt Job? How did Job react?

Job's Defense: Job 29–31

Job feels that he is a righteous man. What is he now saying? Why is he saying these things? Why does Job feel the way he does?

God's Answer: Job 38–42:9

Job was a righteous man who faced some bitter trials. How do you react to God's answer to what Job has been going through? What did God say and do to put Job in his place? How did Job react?

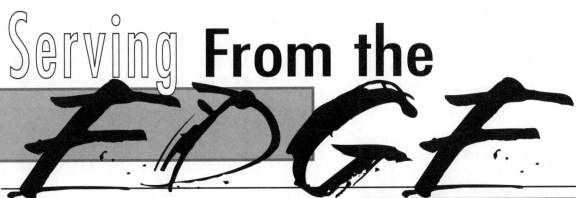
Serving From the EDGE

WHAT'S THE POINT?

Christians are called to serve. This retreat will give the group a chance to explore and experience serving (plan to work on a project together). Many retreat centers will give discounts to groups that do minor repairs, cleaning, or painting around the facility. Another option is to investigate service opportunities in the community where the retreat is being held. Jesus taught us about being a servant and called us to serve. This retreat may inspire the participants to take Jesus' teaching seriously and to serve as he taught.

WHY IT MATTERS

"Whenever you did it for any of my people, no matter how unimportant they seemed, you did it for me" (Matthew 25:40).

OTHER SCRIPTURE REFERENCES IN THIS RETREAT

Matthew 4:18-19
Matthew 5:7-12
Matthew 20:25-28
Matthew 25:31-40
Luke 10:38-42
John 13:1-17
Acts 22:1-21
2 Corinthians 4:8-9
2 Corinthians 11:24

Retreat Schedule

Friday Night

6:00	Arrive and unload
7:00	Meet with group
	—Outline of the retreat
	—Expectations of youth and leaders
7:30	Loopy time
8:30	Break
9:30	Worship
10:30	Bed prep
11:00	Lights out

Saturday

7:00	Get up
7:30	Breakfast/one-on-one time
9:00	Loopy time
10:00	Session 1
11:30	Break
12:00	Lunch
1:00	Session 2
3:30	Free time
5:30	Dinner
7:30	Session 3
9:00	Break
10:30	Worship
11:00	Bed prep
11:30	Lights out

Sunday

7:00	Get Up
7:30	Breakfast/one-on-one time
9:00	Loopy time
11:00	Clean up/pack
11:00	Closing worship

FRIDAY

FRIDAY NIGHT WORSHIP: THE CALL

This worship service shows Jesus calling ordinary people to follow him.

Preparation: Gather several pieces of fishing equipment or other props that can be used to depict ordinary people. Use the props to dramatize the first Scripture reference in Matthew. Modernize the setting if you wish (for example, show Jesus approaching two homeless persons instead of fishermen).

☛ *Open with prayer.*

☛ *Sing* a favorite song or two, such as

= "Screen Door"
= "Let Mercy Lead"
+ "John 12:26: Follow Me"

☛ *Scripture:* Read aloud Matthew 4:18-19 and Matthew 20:25-28.

☛ *Skit:* Have several persons act out Matthew 4:18-19.

☛ *Message:* (*Feel free to expand the following as you feel comfortable.*) Say something like: "Jesus calls us to be a servant and to follow him. The first disciples Jesus called were ordinary people like you and me. They did not hesitate to follow Jesus."

☛ *Discuss* these questions:

• Would you be able to drop everything and follow someone you didn't know?
• Why, do you think, did Jesus select ordinary people?
• What would you have to give up to follow Jesus?
• What are some ways that you already serve others?

SATURDAY

SESSION 1: CALLING ALL SERVANTS

The purpose of this session is to help the participants begin to understand who a servant is.

☛ Have the youth form teams of up to six persons. Assign each team a Scripture passage (see below) that shows Jesus or others serving. After reading their passage the team members are to answer these questions:

• Who are the servants?
• How are they serving?
• What characteristics of a servant are evident?

Possible Scripture passages:

Luke 10:38-42
John 13:1-17
Acts 22:1-21

☛ Have each team present their story and tell what they learned about serving. Encourage the youth to be creative in their presentation. Then have someone read aloud Matthew 5:7-12 to the entire group. Ask:

• What does this passage tell us about the characteristics of a servant?

SESSION 2: THE EXPERIENCE OF SERVING

☞ Devote this time to group involvement in a hands-on service experience. (See notes about possible projects in "What's the Point?" page 51)

☞ After the serving experience, gather the participants and ask:

- How did it feel to be of service?
- Were there moments when it was difficult or challenging?
- How can we serve on a regular basis in our own community?
- How would serving in our own community be different from this experience today?

SESSION 3: SERVANTHOOD ON TRIAL

Preparation: Shortly before the session have a couple of the counselors "arrest" two or three group members who have been caught serving. (For this activity to be effective, conduct the "arrest" and "trial" in as realistic a manner as possible.)

☞ Bring the arrested youth in front of the group (have their hands tied together; they may also look a little disheveled). Present the defendants to the "crowd" and tell why they were arrested. Choose a judge, a prosecution team, and a defense team from the other group members. The remaining participants are to serve as the jury. Give the prosecution and defense teams a few minutes to prepare their case, then let the trial begin. Invite the jury to decide whether the arrested youth should be spared or put to death.

☞ Have someone read aloud 2 Corinthians 4:8-9 and 2 Corinthians 11:24.

☞ Discuss the possible rewards and consequences of serving. Ask:

- What might be some of the consequences of serving today?
- What might happen at school or with your friends if you stood up for an underdog? for someone with special needs? for a group that has experienced discrimination?
- What would you do if you saw a friend harassing another student?
- What are some other situations when serving might be difficult?
- What are the rewards of serving?
- How does service benefit us personally and spiritually?

SATURDAY NIGHT WORSHIP: TO SERVE OR NOT TO SERVE

☞ *Opening Prayer*

☞ *Song:* Sing or play a selection such as + "John 12:26: Follow Me."

☞ *Scripture:* Read aloud Matthew 25:31-40.

☞ *Message:* Recall some times when the group was aware of opportunities to serve. Discuss whether these opportunities were accepted or rejected. (You may also want to draw on examples from your personal experience.) Say something like: "Every time we serve someone else we serve God. Opportunities for service are all around us; there will always be situations and people who can use a helping hand. We simply have to decide which service options we will actively pursue and which we will ignore."

☞ *Self-assessment Activity:* Give each person a pencil and a copy of the worksheet "Matthew's Servant Rules." Allow enough time for everyone to fill out all the items based on the Scripture. Tell the participants to bring their sheets with them to Sunday's worship service.

☞ *Closing Prayer*

SUNDAY

SUNDAY WORSHIP: OPERATION SERVE

Preparation: Have on hand some extra copies of "Matthew's Servant Rules" in case some of the youth misplace their copy or forget to bring it with them. Post a large sheet of paper at the front of the room and provide markers.

☛ *Opening Prayer*

☛ *Play a song*, such as
   = Alrightokuhhuhamen

☛ *Scripture:* Have someone read aloud 1 Timothy 4:12.

☛ *Message:* Encourage the youth to

- be an example to everyone around them
- be willing to give to others
- be open to sacrifice
- be loving to the unlovely

☛ *Call to Commitment:* Have the participants get out their "Matthew's Servant Rules" sheet from Saturday night's worship. Invite everyone to fill out the bottom portion of the sheet ("A Commitment to Serve").

☛ *Invitation:* Invite the group members to approach the large sheet of paper that is posted. The youth are to sign their name and list one or more service projects to which they plan to commit.

☛ *Closing Song*

☛ *Closing Prayer*

Matthew's Servant Rules

How well does your life reflect Jesus' teachings about servanthood as recorded in the Gospel of Matthew? Rate yourself on the statements that follow, using a scale of 1 to 4 (see the key below).

4—This is me.
3—This is often me.
2—This is me on rare occasions.
1—This is never me.

From Matthew 5:7-12:
—— If you are merciful, you will be treated with mercy.
—— If you make peace, you will be called God's children.
—— If you are treated badly for doing right, you belong to the kingdom of heaven.
—— If you are humble, the earth will belong to you.

From Matthew 20:25-28:
—— If you want to be great, you must be the servant of others.
—— If you want to be first, you must be the slave of the rest.

From Matthew 25:31-40:
—— When I was hungry, you gave me something to eat.
—— When I was thirsty, you gave me something to drink.
—— When I was a stranger, you welcomed me.
—— When I was naked, you gave me clothes to wear.
—— When I was sick, you took care of me.
—— When I was in jail, you visited me.

A COMMITMENT TO SERVE

I, _____, commit to doing _____ hours of service over the next six months. I will also strive to improve my servanthood on a daily basis.

Commissioned a Secret Servant Agent on this date: _____

by _____

(Secret Servant Agent Adviser)

Prayer From the EDGE

HAT'S THE POINT?

Prayer is fuel for living. Christians are called to pray in the Spirit. However, many of us don't pray often enough; some youth and adults feel uncomfortable with prayer. The goal of this retreat is to create an environment where youth can learn about prayer and can practice caring for one another by means of prayer.

WHY IT MATTERS

"Never stop praying, especially for others. Always pray by the power of the Spirit. Stay alert and keep praying for God's people" (Ephesians 6:18).

OTHER SCRIPTURE REFERENCES IN THIS RETREAT

Matthew 6:5-9
Luke 18:1-8
Romans 8:15-16
Romans 8:26
James 5:13-18

Retreat Schedule

Friday Night

7:00	Arrive and unpack
7:30	Loopy time
8:00	Session 1
9:30	Break
10:00	Worship
10:30	Bed prep
11:00	Lights out

Saturday

7:00	Get up
7:30	Breakfast
8:30	Loopy time
10:00	Session 2
12:00	Lunch
1:00	Loopy time
3:00	Free time
6:00	Dinner
7:00	Loopy time
7:30	Break
8:00	Session 3
10:00	Prayer vigil (optional)
11:00	Bed prep
11:30	Lights out

Sunday

7:00	Get up
7:30	Breakfast
8:30	Loopy time
9:30	Clean up/pack
11:00	Closing worship

SESSION 1: ALL ABOUT PRAYER

☛ Say a prayer for the success of the retreat.

☛ Introduce the topic by saying something like: "This retreat is all about prayer: what it is, how we do it, why we do it. We will deal with our feelings about praying. Mostly we will practice praying. The simplest definition of prayer is talking or communicating with God. And since the Bible is one way that God talks to us, let's start there. The Bible contains well over three hundred references to prayer. Let's look at some of them."

☛ Have the youth gather in teams of four. Give each team a copy of the "Let Us Pray" worksheet, a large sheet of paper, and markers. (Use the New Revised Standard Version of the Bible for this exercise.) Have each team record their answers on the large sheet of paper. Bring all the participants back together and have each team tell what they discovered. Display the large sheets on the wall so that each one is easily visible.

FRIDAY NIGHT WORSHIP

Preparation: Have two group members work up a brief skit based on Luke 18:1-8. For example, the situation might involve someone (let's call him Chris) "bothering" or pestering another person (we'll call her Tracy) who is not known for her kindness or willingness to help. Tracy finally says yes to Chris's request just to get him to leave her alone.

☛ *Call to Worship:* Sing + "Psalm 71."

☛ *Skit:* Invite the actors to make their presentation.

☛ *Scripture:* Have someone read aloud Luke 18:1-8.

☛ *Song:* Select something worshipful, such as one of these selections:

   + "Lean On"
   = "Creed"

☛ *Closing Prayer:* Thank God for answered prayers. Ask for strength to pray continually and for special insights during this retreat.

SESSION 2: THE LORD'S PRAYER

Preparation: Write the Lord's Prayer (ecumenical text) as follows on a large sheet of paper (or use a more contemporary version if you prefer). Fold up the bottom of the sheet so that it conceals the prayer. Be prepared to reveal the prayer one line at a time.

1. Our Father
2. in heaven,
3. hallowed be your name,
4. your kingdom come,
5. your will be done,
6. on earth as in heaven.
7. Give us today our daily bread.
8. Forgive us our sins
9. as we forgive those who sin against us.
10. Save us from the time of trial
11. and deliver us from evil.
12. For the kingdom,
13. the power,
14. and the glory are yours
15. now and for ever. Amen.

☛ Say something like: "Many Scriptures refer to Jesus' prayers. He prayed to heal others; he retreated to pray alone; prayer was a priority in his life. His followers noticed how focused Jesus was, how prayer provided him with guidance, help, and strength. When they asked Jesus how to pray, he gave them a model prayer, what Christians now call the Lord's Prayer."

☛ Reveal the lines of the Lord's Prayer one at a time. After each line, ask:

 • What do these words mean to you?
 • Why, do you think, was this idea important to Jesus?
 • What other words would you use?
 • What does this line say about God?
 • What does this line say about people?

☛ After reviewing the entire Lord's Prayer, invite all the group members to recite it in unison.

SESSION 3: PRAY IN THE SPIRIT

☞ Start with a prayer asking for God's presence.

☞ Then say something like: "We have touched on some of what the Bible says about the how, what, when, where, and why of prayer. We have noted the power of prayer and the fact that God truly answers prayer. Now let's take a look at how we can apply these learnings to a deeper understanding of what it means to be praying for one another. Pay attention to the first word of the Lord's Prayer (*Our*). When Jesus taught his followers to pray, he taught them to pray together."

☞ Form six teams. Assign the teams these lines of the Lord's Prayer:

    Team A—Lines 1–3
    Team B—Lines 4–6
    Team C—Line 7
    Team D—Lines 8–9
    Team E—Lines 10–11
    Team F—Lines 12–15

☞ Have the teams answer these questions:

- How would we pray these lines as a group?
- How would we pray them for one another?
- What difference would this prayer make in our group?
- What difference would this prayer make in our families?
- What difference would this prayer make at school?
- What difference would this prayer make with our friends?

☞ If your total group is small, combine assignments. If your group is large, label several teams "A," "B,"and so on.

☞ Bring the teams back together. Have each small group tell some key points they discovered. Then invite someone to read aloud Ephesians 6:18.

☞ Ask: How can we commit to caring for one another, supporting one another, praying for one another? (List specific ideas voiced by the group.)

☞ Have someone pray for a spirit of dedication among the group members as they seek to live out the goal of supporting and caring for one another.

PRAYER VIGIL (*optional*)

☞ Invite the youth to express prayer requests. Either record the requests on paper as persons name them, or hand out index cards so the youth can write down their requests. As the sharing draws to a close, give the participants a chance to voice other needs and concerns they are aware of that they would like to bring before the group.

☞ Set a time (perhaps in about thirty minutes) for the group to come back together for a thirty-minute vigil to pray for the above items. Another option would be to end the group time with an all-night vigil. (Before considering this option, keep in mind the ages and personalities of the participants.) You might invite the youth to sign up to pray in shifts throughout the night. Be sure to provide plenty of security for an all-night vigil.

SUNDAY

SUNDAY WORSHIP

☞ *Call to Worship:* Sing + "We Are Grateful."

☞ *Scripture:* Invite someone to read aloud Romans 8:26.

☞ *Prayer:* Allow a few moments for silent prayer.

☞ *Sing* + "Lean On."

☞ *Scripture:* Have a group member read aloud James 5:13-16.

☞ *Prayer:* Solicit prayer requests from the group. Invite one of the participants to pray aloud for these requests.

☞ *Sing* + "You Make Your Home in Me."

☞ *Play* = "Sometimes by Step."

☞ *Scripture:* Read aloud Matthew 6:5-9. End the reading with a group recitation of the Lord's Prayer.

☞ *Closing Song:* Have the participants sing a song that is meaningful to your group.

☞ *Closing Prayer:* End with a circle prayer.

Worksheet

Let Us Pray

Read each of the following Scriptures, then answer the questions:

Matthew 6:5-9
Romans 8:26
James 5:13-18

What do the Scripture passages say about

- when to pray?

- how to pray?

- what to pray?

- what not to pray?

What do you think "with sighs too deep for words" means?

What can be accomplished through prayer?

Where can we find evidence of God's answering prayer?

Healing From the EDGE

WHAT'S THE POINT?

All of us experience various kinds of suffering as part of life, including pain and death. Jesus Christ is our Supreme Healer. This retreat can be an opportunity for the participants to experience healing of sickness and sorrow as a gift from Jesus Christ.

WHY IT MATTERS

"Jesus said to the man, 'Get up! Pick up your mat and go on home.' The man got right up. He picked up his mat and went out while everyone watched in amazement. They praised God and said, 'We have never seen anything like this!'"(Mark 2:10b-12).

OTHER SCRIPTURE REFERENCES IN THIS RETREAT

Matthew 8:1-3
Mark 5:24-34
Mark 10:46-52
Luke 5:17-26
Luke 8:49-56
2 Corinthians 5:17
James 2:14-18

Retreat Schedule

Friday Night

7:00	Arrive and unpack
7:30	Loopy time
8:00	Session 1
9:30	Break
10:00	Worship
10:30	Bed prep
11:00	Lights out

Saturday

7:00	Get up
7:30	Breakfast/one-on-one time
9:00	Loopy time
10:00	Session 2
12:00	Lunch
1:00	Loopy time
3:00	Free time
5:30	Dinner
7:00	Loopy time
7:30	Session 3
9:30	Break
10:30	Worship
11:00	Bed prep
11:30	Lights out

Sunday

7:00	Get up
7:30	Breakfast/one-on-time
9:00	Loopy time
9:30	Clean up/pack
11:00	Closing worship

FRIDAY NIGHT

SESSION 1: HEALING FOR PAIN

☛ To introduce the topic, say something like: "This retreat provides an opportunity to see God work in a powerful way you may never have experienced before. Most of us have endured some kind of pain in our life. We tend to hold on to pain and to keep it locked inside. Jesus frees us to face our pain and overcome its consequences. You and I can be healed of our pain. This weekend we will look at Jesus' healing miracles and discover how healing takes place."

☛ Have the youth work in teams of four to six. Give each small group a copy of the "Jesus Heals" worksheet (circle the verses assigned to that group; more than one team may study the same passage). Allow fifteen minutes for the groups to discuss their Scriptures.

FRIDAY NIGHT WORSHIP

The purpose of this worship experience is to draw the participants into imagining what it would be like to be healed.

☛ *Call to Worship:* Sing one of these songs:

+ "Mercy Me"
= "Verge of a Miracle"

☛ *Scripture:* Have one of the youth read aloud Luke 5:17-26.

☛ *Message:* Invite someone to retell the story of the Scripture in a modern-day setting, or read aloud the following: "Imagine being at a large assembly at school. You're glad to be out of class for a while, even though most of the assemblies at school this year have been rather dull. You walk with your best friend through the crowd of students to the auditorium. You check out the cute guy or girl from your homeroom a little bit in front of you.

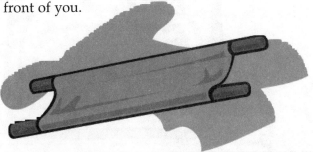

"Then you notice several youth and adults you have never seen before. They seem to be eager to get inside. You start to think that this assembly may be different. Then you hear a loud commotion up above you. You look up and see that someone has broken through the ceiling and is lowering a stretcher into the auditorium. When the stretcher drops closer to the floor, you see a man lying on it. The guest speaker for the assembly walks over to the stretcher. The whole auditorium grows silent. Then the speaker says something to the man. The man stands up, looks at the speaker, and runs out. The crowd erupts in applause. What do you think it felt like to be healed?"

☛ *Song:* Play or sing a song about God's healing touch, such as

+ "Lean On"
= "Awesome God"

☛ *Closing Prayer:* Thank God for miracles, and for the ability to recognize them when they happen. Also pray for insight during this retreat.

SATURDAY

SESSION 2: VISION AND IMAGINATION

Preparation: Write the following entries on a large sheet of posted paper:

    Name
    Town or city protected by super-hero
    Physical appearance
    Special abilities
    Partners or sidekicks
    Mortal enemies

☛ Hand out paper and a pen or pencil to each person. Tell the youth they will have the opportunity to design their own super-hero. Have them write down a description of their hero according to the criteria listed above. Also allow time for the group members to draw their heroes in action. After everyone has finished, invite each person to tell the group about her or his super-hero (if necessary, form smaller teams for discussion). Ask:

• What qualities might enable you to be super-powerful?

- What are your reasons for choosing those particular abilities?
- What would you most like to overcome in your life?

☛ After the discussion, say something like: "The creation of your super-hero took imagination and vision. Those two qualities have a lot in common with faith."

☛ Then have someone read aloud Hebrews 12:1. Say: "In the super-hero activity, you used your imagination to create something. First you had a mental picture, which you then gave form and substance."

☛ Have the group members recall the healing stories from the first session. Ask:

- How did each person who was healed envision his or her future?
- Did that vision change?
- What did the person's vision have to do with his or her faith?
- What did her or his vision have to do with being healed?

NOTE: As part of loopy time in the afternoon, you may want to lead some trust-building activities (see pages 77 and 78).

SESSION 3: FAITH AND RELEASE

☛ Say something like: "We do not get healed without giving up something. All the Bible characters Jesus healed left his presence as different people. They were forever changed because of their experience with him. They all had to leave something behind in order to be changed. Sometimes we get comfortable with a particular lifestyle even if it includes certain problems. We accept that things are just going to be painful and difficult and we forget that life can be better. That is why we need to focus on our vision. Then we can act on our new vision as the next step to healing."

☛ Have someone read aloud James 2:14, 17-18. Invite the group to again recall the stories of healing they considered in Session 1. Ask:

- How did the persons who needed healing show that they had faith? (The woman with the hemorrhage reached out and touched Jesus.)

- How did they know that their actions would lead to being healed? (They didn't know for certain, but they believed that to be the case.)

☛ Form teams of four to six persons (perhaps the same groups from Session 1). Give each participant a copy of the "Turning It Over to God" worksheet. After everyone has filled out his or her sheet, allow about fifteen minutes for the teams to discuss their answers. Keep in mind that these may be tough questions for some of the youth.

SATURDAY NIGHT WORSHIP

Preparation: This worship segment will include praying to God for healing. If this type of service is new to your group, present it in any way that will make the participants feel comfortable. The idea is to provide closeness and support and to demonstrate that God is a healing God. Designate one or more sites as an altar where the group members can gather to pray. Provide metal containers to receive the "offerings" of needs for healing as well as pitchers for water.

☛ *Call to Worship:* Play = "Screen Door."

☛ *Sing* these songs:

+ "We Are Grateful"
= "Sing Your Praise to the Lord"

☛ *Personal Testimony:* Invite one or more volunteers to tell the group about a time in the past when they experienced healing.

☛ *Offering:* Hand out blank sheets of paper and pencils. Invite the youth to write down any difficult situations they are experiencing, painful feelings they are struggling with, or other needs for healing.

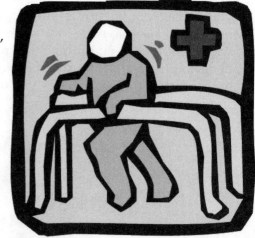

- *Call to Prayer:* Invite the youth to come to the altar one at a time with their paper. As each person comes forward, invite others to place a hand on the participant and pray for him or her. (If the group is large, you might want to have several "praying stations.") Collect the folded-up pieces of paper in a metal container at the altar. After everyone has been to the altar, burn the "burdens" in the pot (only if the setting is safe for this method; be sure to douse the ashes with water). Or you may choose another way to symbolize the burdens being taken away by God.

- *Message:* Say something like: "God has called us to be a loving community of faith. We have offered our prayers to God. We are calling on God's power to heal us. Let us go forth from here a changed people, committed to trusting our burdens to God's power. We seek to truly let go of our burdens and to live more peacefully for Jesus Christ."

- *Closing Song:* Sing = "Awesome God."

SUNDAY

SUNDAY WORSHIP

Preparation: This will be a service of praise and thanksgiving for God's activity in everyone's life. Copy the words to Psalm 149:1-6a, 9b. Divide the passage into about six parts for readers. Have the readers position themselves throughout the group and be prepared to read their verses at the appropriate time. Before worship also ask for volunteers who will tell about some of their personal experiences of God's presence.

- *Call to Worship:* Have someone forcefully read aloud Psalm 150.

- *Sing* a lively praise song such as + "We Are Grateful."

- *Testimonials:* Invite the group members to tell about instances when they noticed God's presence (either during this retreat or at any other time in their life). Start with the volunteers you contacted earlier. Others may also tell their stories and give thanks.

- *Prayer:* Have someone thank God for being present in our life.

- *Praise:* Sing some of the group's favorite songs.

- *Closing:* Invite the designated readers to read aloud Psalm 149:1-6a, 9b.

Worksheet

Jesus Heals

Matthew 8:1-3
Mark 5:24-34
Mark 10:46-52

Read the Scripture assigned to your group, and then answer the following questions:

1. What was the person's ailment or affliction?

2. Consider these possible complications caused by the problem:

    • What about the person's life was different because of having this problem?

    • What practical things did he or she have to do differently because of the problem?

    • What might other people have thought of the main character?

    • How would such reactions affect her or him?

3. What did Jesus do to heal the person?

4. What did the person have to do to be healed?

5. If you had been the person Jesus healed, would you have had enough faith? Why or why not?

Turning It Over to God

1. How does giving up control relate to one's faith?

2. Write down one or more feelings, problems, or situations you are facing that may be causing you pain.

3. Are you aware of anything you can do to ease or solve the situation?

4. Do you believe that God can heal you? Why or why not?

5. What things are keeping you from turning your pain over to God?

Promises From the
EDGE

WHAT'S THE POINT?

Keeping covenants enhances our growth as Christians. The Bible-study format of this retreat provides the framework for a safe environment in which youth can grow with one another. This study will rely heavily on the conversation, questions, and interest of the group members. What Jesus meant when he talked to his followers about a "new covenant" is one core question to consider. In summary, this retreat explores the themes of covenants, commitments, and promises and opens the door to Jesus' new covenant.

WHY IT MATTERS

"And he did the same with the cup after supper, saying, 'This cup that is poured out for you is the new covenant in my blood'" (Luke 22:20, NRSV).

OTHER SCRIPTURE REFERENCES IN THIS RETREAT

Genesis 13
Exodus 3:1-10
Exodus 6:1-9
Exodus 24:3-5
Jeremiah 31:31-34
Luke 20:14-20
Luke 22:19-20
Luke 23:39-43
Hebrews 9:11-14

Retreat Schedule

Friday Night

7:00	Arrive and settle in
7:30	Camp rules and expectations
	Loopy time
8:00	Break
8:30	Session 1
10:00	Break
10:30	Worship
11:00	Bed prep
11:30	Lights out

Saturday

7:00	Get up
7:30	Breakfast/one-on-one time
9:00	Loopy time
10:00	Session 2
11:30	Break
12:00	Lunch
1:00	Group bonding, group adventure, or free time
	—(An afternoon session is another option.)
6:00	Dinner
7:00	Loopy time and/or songfest
7:30	Session 3
9:00	Break
9:30	Worship
10:00	Campfire
11:00	Bed prep
11:30	Lights out

Sunday

7:00	Get up
7:30	Breakfast/one-on-one time
8:30	Loopy time
9:00	Session 4
10:30	Clean up/pack
11:30	Worship

SESSION 1: COVENANTING TOGETHER

☞ Start by saying something like: "I encourage you to approach this weekend with an attitude of discovery. We need to be open to one another's thoughts, ideas, and questions. In that spirit we will start by building a covenant together. A covenant is similar to a contract. A covenant is a binding agreement between two or more parties in the presence of God. A contract or covenant normally has four parts:

- a mediator
- benefits
- expectations
- a response

"In a Christian marriage contract, for instance,

1. marriage is set up by God as the mediator;

2. benefits include being loved, honored, and cherished; having a committed relationship; having a partner for life;

3. expectations include loving, honoring, and cherishing the other in all situations;

4. the response is the affirmation 'I do.'"

☞ Ask:

- Can you think of other contracts that people make?
- Who and what are the mediators, benefits, expectations, and responses in those situations?

☞ Post a large sheet of paper, then ask:

- What contract can we make as a group?

☞ Have the group members brainstorm ideas for a contract. The final draft should be one that everyone can agree with. Keep in mind the goals for the retreat and the four elements of contracts.

☞ Close the session by reading the group covenant together. Then read aloud Luke 22:19-20. Tell the participants that tomorrow they will explore some covenants or agreements found in the Bible.

FRIDAY NIGHT WORSHIP

Preparation: Provide materials for creating symbols of things the youth want to get rid of (anything that may be separating one from God). Have the group members write, draw, or use another medium to express their creativity.

☞ *Sing some songs* that speak to God's power:

- = "Awesome God"
- = "Creed"
- = "Alrightokuhhuhamen"

☞ *Prayer:* Ask God to be part of this worship and the entire retreat.

☞ *Scripture:* Have someone read aloud Luke 20:14-20.

☞ *Message:* Say something like: "Jesus Christ gives us the chance to make a new beginning. At the supper with his disciples, Jesus made clear the opportunity we have to confess to God. Jesus hinted at his own death, which paved the way for every person to start anew. We can die to our old life and begin a new life just as Jesus did at the Resurrection."

☞ *Offering:* Distribute the materials you provided for creating symbols of things the youth want to eliminate from their life. Then have each participant approach a cross and lay down her or his symbol, or burn it up in a fire, or throw it into a trash can. Say something like: "Giving up something can be a freeing experience; it also leaves room for growth."

☞ *Optional Activity:* Lead a Communion or Lord's Supper service. Be sure you know your church's stance on who should officiate at this service.

☞ *Closing Prayer*

Promises From the Edge

SESSION 2: OLD COVENANTS

☞ Have someone again read aloud Luke 22:20. Then ask the group to read together the group covenant.

☞ Say something like: "Jesus mentions a new covenant or new agreement. If Jesus brings a new covenant, what was the old covenant? That distinction is our focus this morning."

☞ Assign these Scriptures to individual youth or to small teams to examine. Have the participants answer the questions that follow.

>   *Genesis 13*
>   *Exodus 3:1-10*
>   *Exodus 6:1-9*
>   *Exodus 24:3-5*

- What covenant is involved?
- Who are the contract partners?
- What are the four contract components?
- Can you tell whether the contract partners are keeping their agreement?

☞ Have the teams report back in the order listed. Then ask the whole group:
- What do these passages tell us about God?
- What do they tell us about human beings?

SESSION 3: PROMISE OF THE NEW

☞ Review with the group the discussions so far. Reread the Luke Scripture.

☞ Then have someone read aloud Jeremiah 31:31-34. Ask the youth to identify the mediator, benefits, and expectations that apply to this covenant. Say something like: "Note that this passage points to Jesus' reference to a new covenant. So the response element did not take full effect until humankind had the opportunity to respond to Jesus' sacrificial love."

☞ On a large blank sheet of paper, write these headings: Mediator, Benefits, Expectations, Response. Then ask:
- What do you know about Jesus' new covenant?

☞ Invite the participants to fill in as much as they know for each of the contract categories relating to the new covenant.

☞ Discuss these benefits if they have not been identified thus far:

1. *Forgiveness of sin.* Read aloud Hebrews 9:11-14. In the old covenant, the high priest offered sacrifices for the sins of the people. The priest acted as a mediator between God and the people. In the new covenant, Jesus Christ acts as our mediator and becomes the "once-and-for-all" sacrifice for us.

2. *Eternal life.* Under the old covenant, God led the people toward the Promised Land. In the new covenant the promise is eternal life to those who stay in right relationship with God. To gain the ultimate benefits of the earlier covenant (eternal life, entrance into heaven), one had to adhere to the numerous laws, rules, and stipulations of that covenant. In the new covenant, qualifying for eternal life still involves being acceptable before God. But we no longer have to rely on our own merits. Jesus' sacrifice for all of humanity became the price of admission to eternal life. We only have to acknowledge and embrace that sacrifice.

3. *Grace.* Grace is God's unconditional love for us. Grace seems to be a new-covenant concept. When people went astray under the old covenant, they would have to do all kinds of things to get back in line with God. In the new covenant, God appears to do all the work. At our birth, we are already given an opportunity to know God; the knowledge is written on our heart and in our mind. God already forgives one's sins through the blood of Jesus. While the Christian life involves certain expectations, these are separate from the element of grace. Our willingness to live in accordance with God's wishes comes from a heart that is being changed by God.

☞ End this session with a review. Note that while the old and the new covenants are different, having a close relationship with God is still the goal. Summarize the progression from one way of thinking to another. Review these elements of the new contract by which we live now:

1. The parties involved are God and all the people of the world.

2. The mediator is Jesus Christ.

3. The benefits are forgiveness of sins, eternal life, unconditional love, and the joys of a personal relationship with God.

4. God has already met the expectations of the new covenant. God, through Jesus Christ, freely offers us a relationship with God. Everything has been provided for us; our only duty is to accept Jesus' sacrifice for our sins.

5. Each person has the opportunity to respond to the new covenant. The response that this covenant deserves from every believer is an honest acceptance of God's free gift.

SATURDAY WORSHIP

Preparation: Have the youth work in three teams to develop a skit, a song, a rap, or some other presentation, based on the three benefits described on page 68 (forgiveness of sin, eternal life, and grace). Encourage the teams to be creative and to use both Old and New Testament Scriptures.

☛ *Songs:* Begin worship around the campfire with these or other songs:

+ "John 12:26: Follow Me"
+ "We Are Grateful"
+ "Remember"
+ "Jesus Is the Rock"

☛ *Presentations:* Have the groups present their creative interpretations.

☛ *Scripture:* Invite someone to read aloud Luke 22:20, then thank God for being in covenant with us.

SUNDAY

SESSION 4: LIVING IN THE NEW COVENANT

☛ Begin by reading aloud Luke 22:20, then have the group recite the covenant they created earlier.

☛ Review the learnings so far. Then say something like: "The benefits of God's covenant with us are wrapped up in a box with each person's name on

it. The box itself is a free gift we call grace, which we can accept or deny. Even if we deny this gift, God continues to offer it. If we accept it right away, we begin to experience the benefits of the new covenant: forgiveness of sin, eternal life, and the joys and peace of a relationship with the God of the universe. When we accept God's grace, our life can change in these ways:

• Our hearts soften.
• We prefer togetherness instead of separations and factions.
• We want honest relationships, not just selfish ones.
• We care deeply about the welfare of others."

☛ Then ask:
• If you accept God's gift, what would your response look like?
• How might your life change?
• What are the responsibilities of a Christian living under the new covenant?
• How can we help one another with the response element of the new covenant?

SUNDAY WORSHIP

☛ *Scripture:* Begin with one last reading of Luke 22:20, then recite together the group covenant.

☛ *Communion:* Invite an authorized person to lead a Communion service.

☛ *Optional Testimonials:* Invite the participants to tell one person or the whole group about any commitments they have made. Offer prayer for any persons who desire it.

☛ *Closing Prayer*

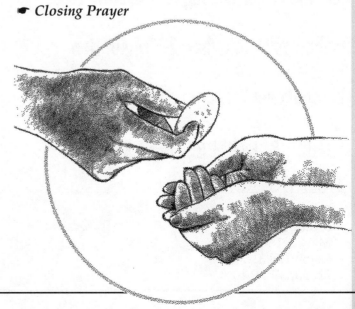

Love From the EDGE

WHAT'S THE POINT?

This retreat is designed to encourage youth to live out the Great Commandment, namely to love God and others. Self-reflection figures prominently in this experience. Activities that stimulate the mind and invigorate the body are also included. Since self-reflection can be difficult for younger teens, this retreat may work best with older youth.

WHY IT MATTERS

"Jesus replied: 'Love the Lord your God with all your heart and with all your soul and with all your mind.' This is the first and greatest commandment. And the second is like it: 'Love your neighbor as yourself.' All the Law and the Prophets hang on these two commandments" (Matthew 22:37-40, New International Version).

OTHER SCRIPTURE REFERENCES IN THIS RETREAT

Exodus 3:1-12
Psalm 139:1-16
Mark 1:16-20
Romans 8:31-39
Romans 10:9-10

Retreat Schedule

Friday Night

7:00	Arrive and unpack
9:00	Session 1
10:00	Self-reflection
11:00	Bed prep
11:30	Lights out

Saturday

7:00	Get up
7:15	Morning devotions
7:45	Breakfast
8:30	Loopy time
9:30	Self-reflection review
10:00	Stretch break
10:15	Session 2
11:30	Free time
12:00	Creative lunch
1:00	Afternoon activities
4:00	Free time
6:00	Dinner
7:30	Session 3
9:30	Campfire
10:30	Worship
12:00	Bed prep
12:30	Lights out

Sunday

8:00	Breakfast
8:30	Morning devotions
9:30	Worship and Communion
11:00	Pack/depart

SESSION 1: DEFINING YOURSELF

☛ Begin by saying something like: "This retreat is about our three most important relationships: our relationship with ourselves, with God, and with people around us. We start with ourselves. Not many people understand that they have a relationship with themselves. It is our first relationship and may be the most important one. When we better understand ourselves, we are more able to grow into the people that God calls us to be."

☛ Have the youth construct bubble gum sculptures. Give each participant several pieces of bubble gum. Invite the group members to open up a piece or two and start chewing. Then give an index card to each person. Invite the youth to use their bubble gum to create a sculpture on the notecard. Each sculpture is to represent something about that person. When everyone is ready, invite the participants to present their "masterpieces."

☛ Then ask:

• If you were to look up the word *you* in the dictionary, followed by your name, what do you think it would say?

☛ Offer a definition of yourself, then instruct the youth to come up with a dictionary definition for themselves. After they have written down a definition, have them find a partner to tell it to.

☛ Call everyone back together. Say something like: "Our priorities are another way to define ourselves. They indicate what is important to us and help determine what we do. Sometimes our priorities are unclear. A few simple questions can help us sort out our priorities. Turn again to a partner and ask each other these questions:

• What do you think about a lot of the time?
• How and where do you spend your time?
• How and where do you spend your money?"

☛ Call the group members back together. Introduce the idea of a silent vigil. While some youth may not relish the thought of a long period of silence, present the opportunity as an exciting challenge. Say something like: "The brief discussion you just had about priorities skimmed the surface of this topic. Tonight you will have additional time to think seriously about who you are. As part of that reflection, we will now begin a silent vigil. From the time this session ends until tomorrow at breakfast, we will all observe a period of silence. While keeping such a vigil may be difficult, I hope you will discover that keeping silent can be a powerful experience."

☛ Give everyone a copy of the worksheet "Me, Myself, and I." Instruct each person to find a quiet place away from the others. The youth are to respond to the questions, statements, and Scripture outlined on the self-reflection sheet. Set no time limit, other than the lights-out curfew.

SATURDAY

☛ Wake the group at 7:00 (or forty-five minutes before time for breakfast). Distribute copies of "One on One: Loving Others." Invite the participants to find a solitary place for personal devotions and to respond to the questions on the worksheet. Then have the youth gather for breakfast immediately following the devotional time. Lift the ban on speech as the group members arrive for breakfast.

☛ Loopy time: Play wake-up games for thirty minutes to an hour after breakfast. The object of these activities is to get the body moving and the participants talking. Try "Dragon's Tail" (page 79) or "Steal the Bacon" (page 80).

☛ Review: Gather the youth back together immediately after loopy time. Say something like: "Let's talk about what you learned from last night's experience and this morning's devotion." Ask:

- Was it easy to stick to the no-talking rule? Why or why not?
- Did you discover anything new about yourself?
- What part of the total self-reflection exercise made the biggest impression on you?
- Have you ever given this much consideration to the various components of your life and your identity before now?
- How do your priorities reflect what is important to you?

☛ End the discussion by reading aloud Matthew 22:37-40.

SESSION 2: "YOU ARE NOT AN ISLAND"

Preparation: Write lunch-time tasks on index cards (one per card). (For example, one person could be in charge of mustard; another one might be responsible for napkins.) Provide for each lunch table a full set of cards covering all the necessary tasks. (If you choose to do so, put tables together. If you have a small group, provide one card for each person.)

This session will focus on how people relate to those around them and on the importance of relationships within a community.

☛ Have the group members stand in a circle. The leader holds a ball of yarn. While holding on to the loose end, the leader gently throws the ball of yarn to another person in the circle. The recipient of the yarn is to tell what gift he or she brings to the group. (If any participant is unable to think of an example, invite the other group members to offer suggestions.) The first recipient holds on to a portion of the yarn and throws the ball to another person. Continue this pattern until the ball of yarn gets to each person once and ends up again with the leader. The final pattern made by the yarn should look something like a spider web. While everyone remains in the circle, ask these questions:

- What does this pattern made by the yarn look like?
- How does this idea relate to us as a group?
- Why is it important to be connected?
- How does each gift we bring contribute to the group experience?

☛ Tell the group that they will have free time until lunch but that they need to gather at 11:50 in order to receive special instructions.

☛ When the participants arrive for lunch, tell them that this meal will be a creative experience. Then hand out the cards. Caution the youth not to look at the cards assigned to the other group members. Then explain that the in-charge person is the only one who can do each task (the "mustard person" is the only one who can dispense and spread mustard for the group).

☛ Proceed with the meal.

☛ After the lunch break, talk briefly about the experience. Say something like: "We are all interconnected. We need one another just to make it through each day. We look to God for guidance, strength, and understanding. God looks to us to be the hands and feet that minister to the world. While such responsibilities are important, this afternoon we will use our spirit of community and togetherness to have some fun."

☛ **Afternoon activities**: If the retreat facility has an initiative or team-challenge course, plan to use it. This is an invaluable tool for creating a sense of community. Instruct the facilitator to work on teamwork and community. If a course is not available, try these games (pages 76–80):

  Willow in the Wind
  Everybody Up
  Trust Fall
  Lap Sit
  Jump Rope
  Off the Ground
  Warp Speed
  Blind Line-up
  Blind Polygon

SESSION 3: LIVING WITH GOD

☞ Debrief the lunchtime and afternoon activities. Then ask:

- How did you see people cooperating?
- How did you see people communicating?
- How did people display their God-given gifts?
- How does a better knowledge of yourself help you be a more effective member of a community?

☞ Read aloud Exodus 3:1-12. Then say something like: "Never again does the Bible mention God speaking from a burning bush. God does not speak to us all in the same ways. Some people hear God through a sermon at church, others while driving a vehicle, some while viewing a sunset or walking in the woods, and still others while reading the Bible. How we act out our faith is different too. The gifts and strengths God gives us are all different. We are to celebrate our differences and learn from them. The most important thing to remember is that all gifts are given to serve God and other people."

☞ Have the youth gather in groups of four and discuss these questions:

- Do you think God loves you? How do you know?
- How do you show that you love God?
- Is Jesus Christ in your life? How?
- If Jesus is not in you life, why not?

☞ Someone in each group is to read aloud Romans 10:9-11. Have the group members discuss these questions:

- What does this passage tell you about God's love for you?
- What difference could that love make in your life?

☞ Next, someone in each group is to read aloud Romans 8:31-39. Have the participants discuss:

- What do these verses tell you about God's love for you?
- What difference would that love make in your life?

☞ Invite the groups to close their discussions with a prayer thanking God for loving us.

Campfire and Worship: Use this time for fellowship, roasting marshmallows, and singing songs.

SUNDAY

After breakfast hand out copies of "One on One: Loving God." Invite the group members to respond to the questions on this sheet during their devotions.

SUNDAY WORSHIP

☞ *Prayer:* Give thanks for the opportunity to spend time with God, with others, and with oneself. Also express appreciation for the learnings and insights gained thus far during this retreat.

☞ *Songs:* Sing some of the group's favorite songs.

☞ *Message:* Say something like: "All relationships—whether with ourselves, with others, or with God—take energy, time, and practice to make them better. I challenge you to see yourselves as important people in the faith community and to nurture a close relationship with God."

☞ *Prayer:* Invite the participants to tell or write down prayer requests. Allow time for both silent and spoken prayers. If you choose to do so, end the worship period with a Communion service.

Me, Myself, and I

Read Psalm 139:1-6, 13-16, then answer these questions:

What is important to you? Why?

What do you think about?

Where do you spend your money? On what do you spend it?

What do you enjoy doing? Why do you enjoy those things?

What do you do that you do not enjoy? Why do you not enjoy these activities? Why do you do them?

Write down three things you hope to be doing in five years.

How do these things fit into your life and activities now? Are you preparing for your goals? How?

What would you say is your highest priority?

How is that priority reflected in the way you live your life?

One on One: Loving Others

One on One: Loving God

Read Mark 1:16-20.

Jesus told his first followers that he would teach them how to reach others. God also calls us to interact in a positive manner with those around us. Take a few minutes to think about your relationships with the people you know best.

What do you like about your family?

What do you like about your friends?

What do you like about your church?

Do you think that your family and friends love you? What is your evidence?

How do you show others that you love them?

How has God called you to minister to the people around you?

Read Matthew 22:37-40.

What does this passage of Scripture say to you?

How does it relate or apply to your life?

What would this passage mean to people you know?

How can you use it in your dealings with others?

What do these verses have to do with our relationship with God?

Do you think God loves you? How do you know?

How do you show that you love God?

Is Jesus Christ in your life? How?

If Jesus is not in your life, why not?

Games From the EDGE

Icebreakers and Warm-ups

Back-to-Back Partner Stand

Have each person in the group find a partner (if possible, the two should be about the same size). The action begins with the partners sitting on the ground back to back. Then they are to  plant their feet, hook their elbows together, and use the other person to push up to a standing position. After all the pairs have accomplished this procedure, repeat the game in groups of three's, four's, and so on.

Curb Shuffle

Locate a log, a curb, a telephone pole, or something else long and thin that the group members can stand on. The idea is for the youth to try to change places without touching the ground. To add an extra challenge, have the participants do this activity without talking.

Everybody Up

Have each person find a partner of about the same height. The two partners then sit on the ground facing each other, with their toes touching and their own ankles together. Using each other for leverage, the partners try to stand up together. A successful attempt finds both persons standing, with toes and ankles still in the original position.

Jump the Peg

This game is a brainteaser of sorts. If there are ten or more persons in your group, try playing a version of "the peg-jumping pyramid" with humans pre-tending to be pegs. Have the youth get in groups of ten. Then ask each team to stand in the following pyramid formation:

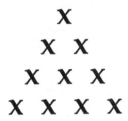

Any remaining members can act as consultants to help figure out the process. The rules are as follows:

Begin the game with one space open (ask one person in the formation to step out). One person in the pyramid moves one step at a time, jumping diagonally or across. A jump can be made only by someone who is next to another participant, with a space on the other side. As a person is "jumped," have him or her sit down to mark that place as an "empty space" in the pyramid. The goal is to leave only one "peg" standing. Play a few times so that the group can gradually learn from their mistakes.

Off the Ground

Have four (or more) persons come to the front of the group. Give them the task of getting all four bodies one inch off the ground for ten seconds. (The hands are the only part of the body that can touch the ground.) One solution is for the participants to sit one behind the other, bending enough to form a circle. Then each person puts his or her feet on the hands of the person directly in front of her or him. All the participants slightly lift their hands, raising all four bodies. The other way is to lie face down in a push-up position. (If there are four doing this, they will form a square.) Each person puts his or her feet high on the shoulders of the person behind her or him. Each person now has someone else's feet on him or her and her or his feet on someone else. Then they all do a push-up.

Touch This Can

Ask for two volunteers of about the same height. Put a soft-drink can between their noses. Everyone else has to touch the can simultaneously without touching anyone else in the group. If you have a large group, try using several partners with cans. If you have a small group, the game will be easy; so after one round, crush the can and have the youth repeat the process.

Traffic Jam

Start with the group in two teams. If you have more than twelve per team, consider having two smaller groups do the same game in different rooms. Have the group start by making two single-file lines with only the first two persons in each line actually facing each other. Have each person stand on a paper plate and place another plate between the two front persons. The object is to have each team change places with the other team. The first person going "north" should end up in the last spot, and the first one going "south" should end up in the other last spot. This is not so easy, because of the following legal (and not so legal) moves:

- Only one person can move at a time.
- One team member cannot pass another.
- No one can move backward.
- Only one person is allowed per space.

Whose Shoes?

Have everyone throw both of his or her shoes into the center of the room. Then each participant is to grab two mismatched shoes belonging to other group members. Now each person, standing in place, must engage in "Twister"-like maneuvers as he or she stretches to find the mate for each shoe and tries to stand up.

You Add It

Have each person find a partner. The partners stand facing each other with their hands behind their backs. At the count of three, they bring their hands out in front of them, holding up any number of fingers they wish. The first partner to add up all the fingers—the combined total from the two—wins the first round. Best two out of three wins. Then everyone finds a new partner.

Trust Games

All Aboard

The object is to get the entire group to stand together on a platform for thirty seconds without anyone touching the ground. Make a box out of wood, or use a stump in the ground (it must be sturdy). With a group of ten to twelve, start with a platform two feet wide and two feet long. Decrease the available space as the group members get better at this.

Blind Line-up

Have the group members gather in a bunch and close their eyes. Provide bandannas for blindfolds. The object is to get the group to line up by height, tallest to shortest, without talking or making noise of any kind.

Blind Polygon

Tie a piece of rope into a loop. Have the youth form a circle and then put on blindfolds. Put part of the rope in each participant's hands. Each person must hang on to the rope with both hands at all times. Then give the group the task of making a square, an equilateral triangle, a polygon, or some other shape.

Electric Fence

Hang a rope between two trees about six to ten feet apart. The rope should be about two and a half feet off the ground. The goal is for all the participants to get over the rope without touching it. They cannot use the trees, or go under the rope. But diving over the rope could lead to injuries. So to make the game a little harder, and safer, have the group members stay in contact the whole time, by touching, holding hands, or some other way.

High-Water Mark

The idea is to get the group to place a piece of tape as high up on a structure as they can. Use an outside wall of a building, a telephone pole, or some other structure that will support people leaning against it. Allow the group members

to use one another to build a pyramid or a human ladder. Those who are not part of the ladder can be "spotters" for the others. This activity is a great one for giving a group a common goal.

Lap Sit

Have the group form a tight circle. Everyone then turns to the right and takes some side steps toward the center in order to create a close configuration. Each person puts his or her hands on the shoulders of the person in front of her or him. (This might be a good time to give brief back rubs.) The goal of this activity is to have the group members all sit down together. Believe it or not, it can be done. Each participant supports the person in front of her or him.

Minefield

Set up an obstacle course using paper plates, balls of all shapes and sizes, socks, pieces of wood, or whatever you have. Mark out an area about 20 feet wide and 40 feet long. Throw all the obstacles or "mines" into the area. Have the group work in pairs, with one partner blindfolded. That person has to walk across the "minefield" taking verbal cues from the partner, who must stay at the starting place. Each touch of a "mine" adds 30 seconds to a participant's time. The fun begins when each blindfolded person tries to cross the obstacle course at the same time.

Trust Fall

Set up a platform about two and a half feet off the ground. Have the group line up (on the ground) in two facing lines, starting at the end of the platform. One person starts by extending his or her right arm, bent at the elbow. The person who is opposite puts her or his right arm next to the first person's. Repeat this pattern until all the group members' arms are interlocked in a catching position. (The end result should look something like a zipper.)

The designated faller (on the platform) then says "Ready to fall." The group, all together, answers back "Ready to catch." The faller responds, "Falling." The group calls back, "Fall." At that point the faller leans back and falls off the platform. Be sure that the faller is standing at the edge of the platform and has his or her heels off just a bit. It is also important to have the faller lead with the shoulders and fall stiff as a board. If he or she falls bottom first, the group might have a hard time catching the person.

Trust Walk

Use caution with any trust walk. One can create a challenging course by having the group go between trees, up stairs, under things, and so forth. Have each person find a partner. One person is blindfolded with a bandanna. The other person takes responsibility for the blind partner. The leader begins the walk and each pair follows immediately after. After a few minutes, have the partners change roles. One other option is to have the whole group (except for one) go "blind" with the "seeing" participant leading everyone else. Whatever arrangement you use, be sure that safety is the first consideration.

Up Chuck

Give each person something to throw, such as a tennis ball or a bandanna tied in a ball. Have the group members gather in a circle and throw their items at least ten feet in the air. The challenge is for each person to catch an item that is not hers or his. Invite the group members to try this a few times, attempting to reduce the number of "drops" each time. Then challenge the group to a "no-drop" throw!

Under the Fence

Set up a string or small rope (about 2 feet off the ground) between two chairs or other objects. Go out 3 feet from each side of the rope and mark a horizontal line with tape or sticks or whatever you have. Now you have a zone that is 6 feet long and a space the group has to pass under that is only 2 feet high. The task is to get the group under the "fence" without touching the rope on the top and without touching the 6-foot space that is marked. Only the group members' feet can touch inside the zone. For a penalty you might make the person start over or put a blindfold on someone. Or feel free to think of an even tougher penalty.

Willow in the Wind

Have the group form a tight circle, shoulder to shoulder. Each person gets in a "spotting" position. Blindfold one person and put her or him in the middle. Have this person follow the commands as described in "Trust Fall." Once the person in the middle falls, the group slowly and lovingly passes that person around the circle. Note that the "faller" must keep his or her heels together and remain still. Allow each person a turn in the middle. If your group is large, some of the participants might "spot" the "spotters"; or form more than one circle.

Other Fun Games

Cold Feet

Provide a big container for each team (buckets or large bowls). Put at least one bag of crushed ice and twenty marbles in each container. Have each team line up behind their container. Tell the teams they will have five minutes to get as many marbles out of their pot as they can, using only their feet and working in relay fashion. The team ending up with the most marbles when time is called, wins.

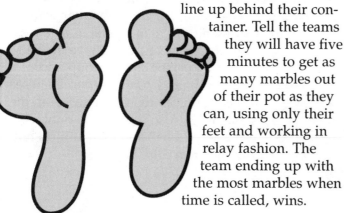

Dragon's Tail

This is a fast-paced warm-up that will get the whole group moving. Place a bandanna in the back pocket of one youth. This person is now the "end" of the "dragon." Have the rest of the group line up in single file, putting the "end" at the back of the line. Each person puts her or his arms on the shoulders of the person in front of him or her. Now you have a long line of people. The person in front tries to retrieve the bandanna from the pocket of the last person in line.

Drink Spittin' Relay

For each team, you will need a milk jug with the opening widened, about two gallons of fruit-flavored beverage, and a small water cooler. The object of this relay is for each group to fill up their milk jug with beverage to a certain point. Place the milk jugs about twenty yards from the groups, and put the water coolers full of drink at the front of each of the small-group lines. The person at the front of each line takes a mouthful of beverage and runs to that team's milk jug. From a standing position he or she must spit the drink into the mouth of the milk jug. (Someone should be at the head of each line to hold up the cooler so that the person going next can get a mouthful of drink while the other person is spitting.) The first group to fill their jug up past the line wins.

Jump Rope

Supply a basic jump rope. The object is to see how many successful jumps a group can make in a row. One option is to have one person jump in, take a few leaps, and jump out, then go on to the next person.

Or try to get the whole group in the middle and see what each person's "personal best" is.

Make Me Smile

Have the group members form two lines facing one another. They should spread out far enough to leave space for a person to walk through this "hallway." Give one person the task of walking down this corridor while trying to keep a straight face. Without touching the walker, the other participants are to do their best to make that person laugh.

Samurai

You will need two foam "pool noodles," each about three feet long. Have the entire group stand in a circle. Place one noodle ("samurai sword") in the middle of the circle. While walking around inside the circle, the leader holds the second sword and announces that anyone wishing to challenge him or her should step out and pick up the other sword. The first of the two opponents to tag the other with his or her noodle is the leader and may then be challenged. The current leader may tag the challenger before she or he picks up the other sword, but standing directly over the other sword to keep it from being picked up is not allowed.

Sponge Toss

You will need two large sponges and two buckets full of water per group. Each team should form two equal lines (or close to it) facing one another. Place one bucket of water containing a sponge at the end of each line. The sponges are to be tossed (the participants may not squeeze out any of the water) back and forth between the lines until they reach the other end. If someone drops a sponge it must be re-dunked in the bucket and started back at the end of the line. Then both lines take a giant step back and begin the sponge toss over again. This is repeated until the distance between the two lines is too great.

Steal the Bacon

Form two equal teams and have them face one another about 20 feet apart. Have the teams number off (for example, if each team has ten players, the members would number themselves 1 through 10). One team should number off beginning at one end of their line, while the other team starts at the opposite end of their line. Place a bandanna in the middle of the two teams. The moderator calls out a number (between 1 and 10 or whatever) and the players assigned that number run to the bandanna and try to bring it back to their line without being tagged by the other player who was called. One point is scored for each return. A tag nets no points. The bandanna is returned to the center and play starts over. Call several numbers at once to create more action.

Warp Speed

Start with several small foam or fleece balls. Have the group members stand in a circle about an arm's length apart. Throw the ball to one person, who tosses it to someone else. Have the ball go to each person in the group once and finally back to the leader. Then see if the group can repeat the tosses in the same order. Also try these variations: Add a second ball and then a third, but throw each to a different person.